EVERYONE SAID
I SHOULD WRITE
A BOOK

Jonathan White

Cover photo: Surviving in the San Blas Islands, Panama., 2001.

Second Edition (2013)

.ISBN: 1468032844
ISBN-13:978-1468032840

DEDICATION

This book is dedicated with love to my traveling partner through life:

Joell Ray Helen White

ALSO BY JONATHAN WHITE

Everyone Said I Should Write Another Book

CONTENTS

ACKNOWLEDGMENTS

Many people have come into my life. Some have moved on, some have stayed. Whether it is a brief encounter of a few minutes or a lifetime friendship, everyone adds something unique to life's experience.

Just a few names here, to those who encouraged me to put my adventures down on paper. Mum and Dad, who wanted me to be a lawyer, but supported my unusual path. Joell my beautiful wife for loving me so much. My brother Grant who is always there for me. Andy Torchon for believing that I should share these stories. Doug Ross for showing me how.

And of course for all the wondrous folks in lands near and far who are a part of the tapestry of my life…

FORWARD

For tall tales, they say, talk to golfers and fishermen. But for true tales of adventure one must go to a seafarer, one with many nautical miles under his keel, lines of spray in his face, and salt in his veins. For he faces the ultimate test of man against the elements, pitting endurance, skill, and adaptability against unforeseen dangers, meeting triumph and disaster and treating them just the same, sometimes living in a day what some of us live a lifetime without experiencing.

I have been most fortunate to have such a man as my older brother. For years I have lived vicariously through his experiences, traveling around the globe to distant countries and tiny remote islands, seeing sights and vistas I shall never see, and truly living a unique life. I have been privileged on a few occasions to join him on the sea and get a small taste of his life – those memories are some of my most treasured, standing out clearly years later.

And through all the years Cap'n Jon has sent back written accounts of his travels, rich stories of triumph over adversity, endurance through hardship, and exotic places and people. He has that rare ability to be able to walk with kings and yet not lose the common touch. Underneath, and running through each story, one sees his firm belief in the essential humanity and compassion that unites us all. Those stories are gathered here together finally – something his family and friends have urged him to do for years – and I am certain you will enjoy them as well. True men of the world are scarce. Here are the adventures of one who Kipling might have used as the model for his poem: If you can fill the unforgiving minute/ With sixty seconds' worth of distance run/ Yours is the Earth and everything that's in it/ And - which is more – you'll be a Man, my son!

Dr. Grant Weiss
Montara, California
December 4, 2011

MY PARTNER

I met my future wife Joell in Marin County, California in the summer of 1996. I was 46, never been married. I knew during our first lunch date that she was the woman I would spend the rest of my life with.

We dated for several weeks, long dinners, driving up the coast in my Bugatti replica, mucking out the stable where Stars her horse lived. We both shared individual passions, me for ocean sailing, Joell for horses and dressage.

I chartered a 30' sailboat in San Diego over the holiday season for a week to see if she liked being on the ocean in a small boat. The first morning out sailing over a sunny, sparkling ocean heading south to Ensenada, Mexico with a couple of dolphins playing around the bow and Enya singing "Sail Away", I asked her to marry me. We had never discussed marriage, she hesitated for only a moment in surprise and said "Yes". Joell loved the experience of moving the boat through the water using only the forces of nature, she loved the excitement of a foreign port and the adventure of sailing off into the unknown. Turned out, she also loved me…

In the spring of 1997 I flew out to North Carolina and bought a 32' catamaran which was transported by truck across the country to Sausalito. She was a rugged, sturdy little coastal cruiser, one of only seventeen custom built in England. Joell and I were married on August 31st, 1997 at my brother's beautiful home on the California coast just south of San Francisco.

Our honeymoon was spent sailing JoJo down to Carmel and Monterey. We made plans for someday voyaging further south. A year after we were married I had a business setback and we found ourselves with a boat and little cash. I landed a job teaching sailing on San Francisco Bay, Joell got a temp job and in our spare time we worked getting the boat prepared to cruise.

Exactly a year to the day after we were married we sailed JoJo under the Golden Gate Bridge and turned left with $900 in our pockets and the unknown before us.

Almost three years, thousands of ocean miles and many adventures later we arrived in Hilton Head, S.C. where I had lived several years earlier. We eventually moved south to Florida, sold JoJo and in 2003 bought a huge, gorgeous and intimidating 64' trimaran which we re-named 'Ladyhawke'. We restored her and sailed back to Panama where we provided luxury charters in the remote San Blas Islands.

Some of the adventures we have had together are recounted in this book including The Pirates of Costa Rica, which was published in newspapers. Some of the tales are of times before I met Joell. All of the stories are true, a couple of the names have been changed but nothing has been exaggerated...

THE PIRATES OF COSTA RICA

We waited aboard JoJo, our 32' Catfisher catamaran along with half a dozen other southbound sailboats anchored in the small, uncomfortable harbour of Huatulco in southern Mexico. Joell and I had just spent a wonderful month in Acapulco and Cuernevaca and were ready to head out to the tranquility and freedom of the open ocean.

Our little group of cruising sailors was about to cross the dreaded Gulf of Tehuantepec, a large exposed body of water separating Mexico from Guatemala and points south. We had been there a few days constantly listening to weather reports. This area is feared by southbound sailors for the sudden hurricane force winds that blow down from the North American landmass and squeeze themselves through a gap in the mountain range lining this coast. Because of the funneling effect of the mountains, the winds (called "Tehuantepecers") and accompanying seas build very rapidly and cause loss of boats, ships and lives every year.

The safest course is to sail cautiously close to the beach over a period of several days about a half mile offshore and do it as quickly as possible, for there are no protective harbours on this coast. But some more intrepid sailors opt to head offshore and make the 250-mile open ocean passage across the Gulf in two or three days. After listening to U.S. weather forecasts we all decided that tomorrow would be a good time to leave.

The next morning seven sailboats headed out with a brisk WNW wind blowing. Six of the yachts turned left and sailed close inshore intending to cross the Gulf with 'one foot on the beach'. JoJo alone headed straight out at a spanking seven knots with sails pulling beautifully, full tanks of diesel and plenty of provisions aboard. Our plan was to bypass Guatemala, El Salvador and Costa Rica and sail directly to Panama.

The first day and night were magnificent with a constant 20-knot wind over the quarter, comfortable motion and delicious temperature. We looked forward to a speedy and glorious ten day passage as long as the conditions held.

By the next morning it was apparent that they wouldn't as the wind kept dropping and dropping until it stopped blowing at all. Within a few hours the seas were flat calm and the sun was boiling hot. We didn't carry nearly enough fuel to motor the almost one thousand miles to Panama but on went the diesel at low rpm and we chugged across a hazy, hot, barren sea at a sedate four knots to conserve fuel.

Day after blistering day and night after magic night there was nothing to be seen except the horizon and occasional floating patches of garbage. Once we came close to a seagull apparently standing on the surface of the water in an area where the ocean is very deep. We altered course to come closer and found him preening while balancing on the back of a sleeping turtle!

After six days I began to worry that we would run out of fuel so we decided to head to Costa Rica. We altered course to the east but still had two hundred miles to go.

The following day as we putted along at 1000 rpm, I was on watch and did a visual sweep of the horizon. Having not seen another ship since leaving Huatulco I was excited to discern a speck on the eastern horizon. After a few minutes my binoculars showed that the vessel was heading directly toward us, about 8 miles away. I tried to raise her on the VHF radio with no luck.

As she came closer I could see that she had no mast, so was not another sailboat but probably a local freighter or fishing boat. It was apparent after about fifteen minutes that she was still headed directly for us. Knowing that local boats keep a sketchy lookout at best I reluctantly pushed up the throttle so as to allow her plenty of room to pass astern. But she changed course to intercept us.

At this point there was no doubt in my mind that she was purposefully heading directly for JoJo and had no intention of passing us. She seemed to be a fishing boat about 40' long with nets and floats hung haphazardly on her decks. She was seedy-looking, in need of paint and was blowing clouds of black smoke from her exhaust which signified to me that the engine was revving high and she was moving quickly.

I woke Joell who was sleeping in the salon and told her we were about to have visitors, possibly not friendly. I hailed them on the VHF radio but there was no response. By this time they were about 300 yards off our port beam and had slowed their boat down to keep pace with us.

As they edged closer I hoped they just wanted some cigarettes or a bottle of rum. Joell however was not so sure about their intentions and she decided to disguise herself. Hurrying below she donned a heavy jacket and bunched her hair under a hat. Standing in the companionway door, she looked like a large man.

Now the 'fishing boat' was only 200 feet away from us and all of a sudden four dirty, disheveled, tough-looking men emerged from the wheelhouse and lined up on their starboard side with not a smile amongst them. They just stood there looking at our boat and us two gringos, a hundred miles from land with no one else in sight.

I got on the VHF and started calling "Mayday, Mayday" but as the VHF has only a twenty mile range I had little hope of raising another ship. A voice responded on the radio, sinister and slurred:

"Hey, Capitan, waz de problem? We jus' pescaderos, no hay problema."

I responded in my elementary Spanish, "Ah, bueno, todo bien?"

"Si, Capitan, todo bien. You has nice yate and we jus' pescaderos."

Maybe we weren't about to be attacked, maybe they really were just pescaderos, fishermen, but we didn't like the way they never took their eyes off us or our beloved JoJo as they kept pace a couple of hundred feet away. Then they sped up and pulled ahead, crossed our bow and did a complete circle of us.

I have never felt more vulnerable in my life, even being shot at in the Khyber Pass or close to death with dysentery in the Himalayas. We were totally at their mercy and for the first time, we wished we had a firearm on board.

But then they grinned evilly with many a gap in their teeth and steamed off westward over the horizon. Feeling shaken and scared we sat in the cockpit and discussed how we could protect ourselves should something like this ever happen again.

We took stock of what we had aboard; the flare gun with six flares, fire extinguishers, barbecue lighters, spear guns and small gasoline jugs for the outboard. I explained to Joell that in a last ditch situation we could make Molotov Cocktails by filling glass jars with the gasoline, stuffing rags in them for wicks, lighting them and throwing them at an aggressor.

Still concerned but feeling slightly more secure Joell took off her heavy clothes and went back to an uneasy sleep in the salon. I felt the wind finally trying to assert itself and scanned the horizon every few minutes. About an hour later I saw a speck on the horizon to the west, the direction the 'fishermen' had gone. The speck got bigger and bigger and I silently prayed it was coincidental and this was a freighter or cruiser. As it got closer I could see the black spume of smoke and there was no doubt about it – they were back and heading straight toward us…

Hurriedly rummaging in the big locker, I dragged out our two small gasoline cans. Joell began emptying bottles and jars of their contents and thrusting them at me to fill with gas. The wind started to blow a little stronger, causing wavelets that slopped gasoline all over the cockpit. I stuffed towels and rags in the jars, looking over my shoulder constantly at the approaching boat. I managed to get a few "Mayday" calls out on the VHF but there was no response – we were definitely on our own and very vulnerable.

They came dangerously close and I was visibly shaking though trying not to show it. The captain called to us that we had nothing to fear, they were just 'pescaderos'. So why did they choose exactly the same spot in the ocean that we were? I pushed the throttle to maximum, the little Yanmar diesel straining to get us to seven knots, gulping our precious reserves of fuel. I changed course, they sped up and followed us about 100 feet away.

The wind started to kick up, the waves were building. I clambered onto the cabin top and hoisted the mainsail, Joell steering the boat into the wind. With the main up, I skidded back into the cockpit sliding on the spilled gasoline, unfurled the jib, sheeted the sails in and we picked up speed, quickly doing nine knots.

I tacked and tacked again, the pirates getting confused over what we were doing. They hit their throttle but slowly, ever so slowly, with our engine screaming and sails pulling, yard by yard, we moved away from them.

The wind got stronger, JoJo cutting twin swaths through the waves, sails pulling, us smiling, faint with relief, the 'fishing boat' slowly receding into the distance. After two hours they were no longer in view, I throttled back the engine, we eased the sheets and set a course for Costa Rica, about fifteen hours away. We were tired, scared, relieved and safe.

After a bizarre night with strange lights all around us, vivid green shapes pulsing just under the surface and glittering stars overhead we tied up at Flamingo Marina in the morning to take on fuel – we had enough for about an hour motoring left in the tank!

We believe the universe was looking after us, providing the wind we needed so desperately after a week of flat calm...

Were they pirates or just fishermen who saw an opportunity out in the middle of the ocean? We didn't know and didn't stick around in Costa Rica to find out...

AFGHAN DILEMMA

I sat in the back row of the rusty, creaking Japanese minibus as we bounced our way across the bleak Afghan desert from Kandahar to Kabul. In front of and next to me, their turbaned heads brushing the roof were seven Afghan tribesmen complete with ancient carbines and crossed bandoliers.

They talked amongst themselves and occasionally cast a glance back in my direction. Although there were a number of young westerners on the 'hippy trail' in that fall of 1971 this was probably the first time that a lone 'ferengi', complete with bushy beard and long hair traveled beside them. I was on my way to meet up with my friends who were already in Kabul. Foregoing my usual hitchhiking as the weather was turning cool, I had found this minivan in a small market area in Kandahar a couple of hours before. For two dollars I would be in Kabul soon. By now I was immune to the pervasive odour of unwashed bodies and uncured, dirty sheepskin coats emanating from my traveling companions.

It was the beginning of Ramadan, the holy month for Moslems; for thirty days they don't eat from dawn to dusk. I knew this but reached into my pack and brought out some crusty bread and goat cheese. Seven long, gaunt, slightly hostile faces turned toward me...

"Oh", said I, slapping my forehead, "Ramadan!"

I made a big deal of putting my food back into my pack, the tension was gone and they smiled good-naturedly.

These were the descendants of some of the fiercest warriors the world has ever known. They had withstood invading armies from Genghis Khan to the British Empire and would eventually defeat the Russians. It was said that if you were wounded in battle against the Afghans, it would be much better if you died, because

9

when their women scoured the battlefield afterwards they would do unspeakable tortures to an enemy left alive. They were tall, fierce-looking, proud, dirty and looked capable and very eager to protect their barren lands.

Suddenly there was a loud bang, the bus lurched to one side and we rolled to a stop. Everyone piled out to inspect the flat tyre. The driver cheerfully threw the baggage piled in the back onto the roadside, rummaged around to find his tools and the spare and went to work. It was cold in the desert and within three minutes one of the men had built a warming fire, made with dried camel dung patties found beside the road.

Perhaps because of my gesture with the food they seemed to be comfortable with me; one of them spoke a few words of English. Using hand motions and a stick in the sand I tried to explain to them how big a skyscraper is and that there are tubes under the ground through which people hurtle in metal trains. Supermarkets, redwood trees, sailboats, these and more were 'discussed' and marveled over with looks of wonder and disbelief.

A few minutes before we were ready to squeeze back into the van we stood around smoking, as I shared my cigarettes with them. One man, the one who spoke a few words of English pointed to himself and told me his name was Ali. I told him mine. He then pointed to himself again and said clearly,

"Ali, Moslem – Jon, Christian?"

A defining moment in the life of a twenty-year old! How do I answer this question here in the middle of nowhere, no one knowing where I was, surrounded by these gun-toting tribesmen?

In a sudden flash of insanity I decided to be truthful. Standing tall, with them waiting expectantly for an answer, I looked Ali squarely in the eye, pointed to myself and said one word,

10

"Jew."

After I said it I had this momentary vision of seven ferocious Afghanis gleefully dismembering me with their deadly knives and leaving me to rot in the desert.

A startled look came into Ali's eyes and he walked quickly around the fire toward me. I stared back at him unflinching as he rushed up and stopped inches from me.

He studied me up and down, an intense look of disbelief on his face. I glanced behind hoping for an escape route but the others had moved closer to me, their eyes unwavering. For ten seconds no one moved. My mind raced as Ali raised his arms at me. I expected a blow and automatically started to shield my face.

Instead of hitting me, he threw his arms around me. He hugged me tight and his bad breath overpowered me.

He stepped back and spoke only one word,

"Bruzzer!"

I was taken by surprise and immensely relieved. He talked rapidly to his friends who looked at me with amazement, all gesturing wildly with their hands. One by one they shook my hand, told me their names and smiled at me. We sat down around the fire, joined by the driver who by now had replaced the flat with a bald spare tyre. Ali explained haltingly in a few words his reaction to my confessing to being a Jew in this apparently hostile environment.

"Abraham, Moslem father; Abraham, Jew father - we bruzzers."

Here at the ends of the earth, warming ourselves by a camel dung fire was this simple man's profound understanding of men's real relationship to each other. He wasn't concerned with the rhetoric of modern politicians; he probably couldn't even read a newspaper. But he did know that five thousand years ago, we both came from the same patriarch and in spite of our vast differences we were indeed brothers...

BARNACLE BILL

"Have you seen a little green parrot?" asked Brandon.

The precocious seven-year-old was running down the docks stopping at every boat, looking quite distraught. His grandfather Bob had his boat moored next to us at the funky Marina Nautico in Cartagena, Colombia. Brandon and his two brothers had flown down from Los Angeles for a visit and Bob had bought them a little parrot from a local who had wandered into the marina with half a dozen birds in tiny cages. The kids were getting bored and the parrot had provided them with entertainment for the past three days.

But now they'd lost him and there was a frantic search, including scanning the water. I suggested we thoroughly search Bob's boat and as we went aboard the oldest brother called out from below that they had found him. The poor little thing had wandered down into the engine room and was wading around in two inches of oily bilge water! After some dexterous maneuvering he was gently captured and brought onto the dock where he was carefully hosed off and cleaned. At this point he started shaking and displayed an overall miserable demeanour.

Seeing the little blighter's distress we put him in his cage (which we had insisted they buy for him the day before) and took him to our boat. Joell used to be a zoo keeper and she had also volunteered at Wild Care, a bird rescue centre near San Francisco. We covered the cage and forbade anyone coming aboard for twenty-four hours. We didn't have much hope for him as he was forlorn and scared and we felt sure he would die.

However his will to live was strong and the next day he was perky and curious. We fed him well and protected him from being handled by the kids. Over the next few days he grew stronger and we grew attached to him. Whenever something would happen he would chirp "Oh, Oh!" and crack us up. The kids lost interest and we became the parents of 'Barnacle Bill', the parrot.

It was obvious that this was a bird which had been captured in the wild as they are not bred here. Bill had a wonderful temperament, was funny and talkative. He would say "OK" and almost "What a pretty bird". We would take him down to our cabin and let him walk all over us and pull our hair. But it was apparent that he was not happy…

A week after he became part of our family we had hauled our boat to have her painted in a local boatyard. There was a large tree just outside the yard with hundreds of small, green parrots roosting in the branches. In the mornings and evenings they would fly around; Barnacle Bill would screech at them and they would collectively screech back – it was quite heartbreaking.

During the next few weeks Bill's flight feathers grew back and he took to flying around the salon whenever he could. At first he would flap vigourously and plummet down but eventually he started flying around and up. He also became noticeably less friendly toward us and pecked furiously at his mirror.

It was obvious that he could now fly and he showed a tenacity and strength of character that made us sit down to discuss his future. We decided that if he was given the choice to remain caged up or take his chances in the wild, he would vote for freedom.

We spent the night at anchor and the next morning, the last day we would be in Cartagena, we got up at 5:00 a.m. We covered his cage with a T-shirt, climbed into the dinghy and putt-putted to shore. There we hailed a sleepy taxi and drove to the 'parrot tree', near the boatyard.

Hundreds of little green parrots were circling and calling out and Bill screeched back to them.

We set his cage near the tree and opened the door. He looked confused for a few moments, ran around his cage then slowly climbed out. Within a second he had spread his wings and flapping furiously, flew around us once and headed off to the tree singing at the top of his voice…

BAPTISM BY GALE

I had just finished an early dinner with Joell and Mum (who was visiting) on our catamaran JoJo in Ventura Harbour, California, where we were then living. We had left San Francisco a few months earlier and I had secured a position as a captain for Vessel Assist (VA), the maritime equivalent of AAA, two weeks before. I was about to suggest a quiet game of Scrabble when the VHF radio became active on Channel 16.

It was my boss Dave Delano, the owner of the Vessel Assist franchise which covered the waters from Point Conception south to Oxnard. We switched to a working channel and he told me a commercial fishing boat was adrift north of Santa Rosa Island and was in need of immediate assistance. Even though I had been working for only two weeks and had limited experience on the 'AVTA', the old 33 foot Owens twin-engine cabin-cruiser/towboat, it was apparent that I would be called to this rescue - Donnie the primary driver, was on his way to an EMT class.

I quickly gathered my gear, Joell stuffed some sodas and bananas into my bag and I ran the half mile to the VA dock and the boat. Dave met me there and had already paged my crewman Rob. I ran down the ramp to the dock, started the engines, switched on all the navigation and communications equipment and did a quick visual check. I hurried back up to the cramped office to gather as many details as I could about the position, size of the vessel in need of assistance, sea conditions and rate of drift.

The distressed boat was equipped with a GPS so I had an accurate position fix, which put him about nine miles north of Santa Rosa Island, a distance of about fifty miles from Ventura Base. The small boat, named 'The Office' was a 24-foot Radon, a sturdy, one-man commercial sea urchin fishing boat and the captain had reported to the Coast Guard that the sea conditions were moderate with a 2-3 foot chop. Little did we realize that those conditions were about to change radically and rapidly...

Rob cast off and I motored slowly away from the dock sitting up on the fly-bridge enjoying the magnificent scenery of the mountainous backdrop, the clear blue sky and the hundreds of boats securely tied up in the marina. Having entered the Radon's position into my onboard GPS, the resulting computation showed that my target was exactly 47.8 miles away.

With a cruising speed of fourteen knots, I radioed the Coast Guard control centre in Long Beach that I would arrive on site to take the Radon in tow in approximately three and a half hours, an ETA of 22:00 hours (10:00 p.m.). I then called my wife on the VHF radio to let her know that the weather conditions were getting a little blustery and not to expect me back until the early hours of Friday morning.

The first indication that the weather was about to change was a sudden, fierce gust of wind from the northwest as I turned AVTA left into the channel leading past the breakwaters into open ocean. I quickly left the fly-bridge and returned to the inside steering station where I was to spend the next seven exhausting hours glued to the radar, GPS and VHF radio. Leaving the protection of the breakwater wall it became apparent that the wind was picking up rapidly - seas were already forming and were three to four feet with whitecaps.

Dave called me on the cellphone from his car on the bridge between Ventura and Channel Islands Harbour to let me know that he had just been buffeted by the building winds. He suggested that rather than steer a direct course to my target into the quickly building winds and seas, I alter course to the Anacapa Passage. I should then steer along the south side of Santa Cruz Island and make a strategic course decision in a couple of hours. My choices at that time would depend on where the Radon had drifted.

17

Even though I have many thousands of ocean miles under my belt, these waters were fairly new to me. Joell and I had sailed our 32-foot Fisher catamaran JoJo down to this area from San Francisco in October of 1998, had cruised the north side of Santa Cruz Island and around Anacapa Island but basically I was heading into unknown territory - at night, in swiftly deteriorating weather and on an old boat I hardly knew.

Rashly ignoring Dave's advice I turned the bow of AVTA west toward my destination and into the wind and seas - not a good idea! We were instantly slammed as the bow rose and fell heavily in the short, steep chop. I quickly altered course to the East End of Santa Cruz Island and the Anacapa Passage as the sun set, the skies grew darker and the wind and waves picked up. Tuning the VHF radio to the weather channel I heard imminent gales forecast up and down the coast.

What was initially a routine rescue now had more ominous and dire overtones. With the increase in wind and waves the lone fisherman in his small boat was being inexorably pushed toward the rocky reefs off the northeast point of Santa Rosa Island...

I told Rob we were in for a long night but we were both in good spirits and anxious to do our respective jobs well. The Coast Guard in Long Beach had strong radio contact with 'The Office' but I was unable to converse with him directly at this distance.

Coast Guard Group Long Beach had set up a VHF radio schedule with the fisherman - they would call him every half-hour for a position update and to let him know my ETA. They also set up a radio schedule to monitor my progress. Because of the longer distance I now had to travel I changed my ETA to approximately 2330 hrs. (11:30 p.m.). The Coast Guard informed the fisherman and he told them that his rate of drift had increased with the onslaught of the gale.

The wind was continuing to increase and the boat was rolling heavily as I rode the swells and waves toward the lee of Santa Cruz Island. It was pitch black out and the windshield wipers were useless in combating the water pounding the forward windows. As we raced toward the Anacapa Passage at fourteen knots I anticipated that the seas would diminish as we found protection along the south side. This proved accurate but the 32-year old AVTA still felt the effects of wind rushing over the island and creating large seas even in the lee.

Ahead was a very bright light, the type of intensity that only a squid-fishing boat could produce. The boat slowly came abreast as we pounded our way up the coast, showed up on the radar screen as a target and moved behind us. Suddenly, there was a dim flashing light directly ahead, barely visible through the sheets of spray and rain.

I quickly scanned my chart and found small Gull Island approximately one and a half miles south of Santa Cruz Island, directly in my path. While trying to keep my wildly fluctuating flashlight beam steady on the chart I noted that there is a ten second flashing light with sixteen mile visibility in perfect conditions - these were far from perfect conditions!

The only way I had been navigating along this rugged coast was to use the radar to stay about one mile off, reasoning that the islands are steep-to and I should be clear of any dangers. Rob and I started to count the time interval between the flashes and independently came up with a five-second light, not ten seconds as the chart indicated. I was getting a little concerned, kept checking my position on the GPS relating it to the chart (not easy in a madly pitching boat) and looking earnestly at the radar screen searching for the blip that would be Gull Island.

I had just altered my course ten degrees to port to give myself a wider margin when Donnie's voice came over the VHF speaker.

He sounded quite cheerful (understandably so, he was at home!) and wanted to know how we were doing. I explained to him that there was a five-second light just off our starboard bow and I had no such light on my chart. He responded that he wasn't sure of the correct interval but that he would check and get back to me. Right then another voice (later ascertained to be a Harbor Patrolman) cut in informing me that it was indeed a ten-second light.

Now we were perplexed- where exactly were we relative to Gull Island? Just at that moment the island showed up on the radar screen as a distinct landmark separate from Santa Cruz Island. There was no doubt that the flashing light we were seeing was on Gull Island, even though the sequence was different. I informed Donnie that we were just off the island proceeding at about twelve knots in zero visibility. Two minutes later the Coast Guard called 'The Office' for the scheduled 2230 hours radio contact.

When the fisherman responded with his position I was able to pick him up on my radio which indicated that he was closer to me. After punching his coordinates into my GPS it was apparent that he was drifting at about two miles per hour and was heading for Fraser Point and the shallow waters off the extreme northwest tip of Santa Cruz Island. Our decision was made for us and I plotted a course to take us through the channel between the two islands. Donnie came back on the radio to inform me that the seas which were already large, would become more so as we rounded Gull Island and set off through the channel. His exact words were:

"I'm not going to sugarcoat it for you - it's going to get even rougher!"

He advised me to keep closer to the shore of Santa Rosa Island, that the passage was clear of obstructions and I shouldn't hit anything "that goes bump in the night!"

Just then the fisherman called on the VHF with a little fear in his voice and asked that we get to him as soon as possible as he felt he would be on the rocks in less than an hour...

As we turned to starboard to position the boat for its run down the channel, the seas felt much bigger and the wind picked up its intensity. The night was pitch black and nothing could be seen through the windshield which was being pummeled with sheets of water every time we jumped off a wave. I pushed the two throttles forward and with my eyes glued to the radar, told Rob to hold on.

The boat speed climbed to sixteen knots and we were taking a beating. I was driving blind through the night, through the gale, through the waves with nothing but the throbbing sound of the diesels in my ears and the eerie pale glow of the radar for company.

Water cascaded over the boat, Rob and I were battling to hold on, prudence dictated throttling back, but there was a lone fisherman helplessly being pushed toward the rocks and almost certain death.

For the next thirty-five minutes my eyes were locked onto the radar and the GPS. I was aware of nothing except the fierce, pounding motion, the water leaking around the old windows, the crashing of the boat through the waves and Jethro Tull playing 'Locomotive Breath' in my brain - it was indeed a 'shuffling madness'...

I received a position update from 'The Office' which showed him about two miles ahead of me - he figured he'd be on the rocks in half an hour at his current rate of drift. I requested that he give me a 'ten count' in order for me to get a radio 'DF cut' which then enabled me to obtain a line of position on him.

The adrenaline was pumping fiercely now and as we came out of the limited protection formed by the lee of Santa Rosa Island the seas got even bigger. I radioed 'The Office' that I would be on site with him in a matter of minutes and he sounded relieved. But we were not out of the woods (or rocks) yet!

It's not easy to locate a small vessel in appalling conditions like these. I thought I had him on the radar but couldn't be sure if the fuzzy blip was his boat or a large wave. I told him I would switch on my powerful forward lights in the hope that he would see me.

"Yes," he shouted through the radio, "I see you to the south of me less than a mile away."

"OK," I responded over the VHF, "Flash your lights for me."

"There he is," yelled Rob, pointing ahead through the water-streamed windshield.

"Where?" I called back, struggling with the helm.

"Straight ahead, real close."

As I throttled back to come in near to him, the size of the seas became apparent. We were in shallower water and they reared up in a confused manner pushed by fifty-knot winds. He opened the companionway door leading to the deck and the wind howled and pummeled us. Within seconds Rob was soaked by blowing spume. He clawed his way to the aft deck and prepared to clip the tow hook to the bow of the Radon.

Fifteen seconds after he was on deck a large wave broke behind the boat, soaking him in cold seawater. The fisherman turned on his running lights and his cabin light which gave me a clearer target.

Now I had to back down on him in twelve-to-fifteen foot steep seas and hold my wildly bucking boat steady while Rob attempted to hook the towing clip through an eye on the front of the Radon (lesson learned here - in these conditions, don't do it this way...).

Three times I maneuvered the stern of AVTA to within feet of the bow of 'The Office', with Rob leaning over the transom to hook the eye. The seas were confused, steep and curling. I yelled to Rob that the fisherman had to come on deck, for Rob to throw him the towline and for the fisherman to lean over the bow and clip the towline on. Rob screamed back to me that it would be suicide for the fisherman to come onto his small and cramped foredeck and that he would try to hook the boat again. At this point we were perfectly lined up with the bow of the Radon about four feet off my stern. Rob leaned out with the pole and all of a sudden a huge wave lifted the Radon behind us.

In slow motion, 'The Office' towered above us and assumed a thirty degree angle on the face of the wave, her pointed bow aimed straight at our vulnerable transom.

I shoved the gears into forward and slammed both throttles to their stops, yelling for Rob to watch out. Because AVTA was so much heavier she didn't respond as quickly to the wave. Just as our propellers bit and we started to move forward I looked behind and saw the Radon shoot down the wave and slam into us with a resounding crash and AVTA shuddered from the blow…

Rob had managed to scramble out of the way and was shaken but not hurt. The night was pitch black, the wind was howling, the rain was pelting and I thought we had been holed. From my position at the helm, looking back it appeared that his steel anchor roller had pierced us below the waterline. All I could think was that we would likely sink in a few minutes…

"Are we holed, Rob?" I screamed at him, my voice battling the wind.

He ran to the stern and looked over as the boat bucked and reared in the steepening waves.

"Yes," he yelled back. "Yes, we are."

"Is it below the waterline?" I screamed again.

"I don't know; it's hard to tell in these waves. Wait, OK, I can see it now, it's about a foot above the waterline, about the size of my fist!"

I scrambled quickly to the stern, shone my torch over and saw a five-inch hole with jagged fiberglass around it. But it was higher than the red antifouling paint which meant it was above the waterline.

I felt relieved although a lot of water could still flood in. I looked around for the Radon and saw it about a hundred yards off, its lights dimming as the batteries lost power. I had to get to him before his lights went out or it would be impossible to find him again.

I quickly opened the engine room hatches and saw about six inches of water sloshing around the bilge. I shone my torch onto the bilge pumps and could see they were working, sucking water over the side, staying ahead of the incoming flow. I slammed the hatch closed and jumped back inside to the wheel.

"OK, Rob," I yelled. "I'm going back to him. We've got one shot. I'm going to call him on the VHF and get him on deck. As soon as you can, toss him the line then yell at me when he has it – OK?"

Rob looked scared and was shaking but he coiled the tow line and positioned himself. I called the fisherman on the VHF and he agreed with my plan.

As I circled back through the waves I could see him make his way from his tiny cabin out to the bow of his boat, keeping low. I reversed up to him and Rob leaned over and extended the pole with the towline attached to it. I had assumed that he would have disconnected the pole and just tossed the line to the fisherman but he hadn't. The pole was snatched out of his hand with the desperation of a drowning man clutching a straw. I thought that the cliché was appropriate in these circumstances...

The fisherman detached the line and tossed the pole aside. Leaning over the bow he quickly attached the tow clip, gave a thumbs-up and edged his way back into his cabin. From arrival on-site to hook-up had taken about twenty minutes. With Rob paying out the towline, I glanced at the radar. We were less than half a mile from the reefs off Fraser Point. I looked at the depth sounder-it showed only sixteen feet! We were in immediate danger of being swept ashore and in these conditions none of us would survive...

I yelled at Rob to secure the towline as we needed to get out of there fast. He shouted back that we were ready to go. I gave the boat some throttle and the sound of the engines increased. I was glued to the radar, watching to see us edge away from the land – it wasn't happening...

I thought for a panicked moment that we were caught in a strong current that swept around Fraser Point and was pulling us relentlessly toward the rocks. Reaching down to give us maximum throttle I noticed that I had neglected to put the gear controls from neutral to forward!

Feeling stupid but relieved I jammed the throttles back to idle, pushed the gear levers forward and moved the throttles quickly back to twelve hundred rpm. With eyes back on the radar I watched the island very slowly moving away but it was soon apparent that the wind and waves were combining to push us southeast toward the rocks.

I altered course to the northwest and pushed the throttles up another two hundred rpm. The next ten minutes were spent intently staring at the radar, the GPS and the depth sounder to determine our speed and course. We slowly clawed our way off the dangerous lee shore and I punched in the coordinates for Santa Barbara Harbour, our destination.

It was now just past midnight and the GPS showed that at our rate of speed (about five knots under tow) we'd be off the harbour entrance at about 5:15 a.m. I radioed Coast Guard Long Beach and informed the competent woman who had been my liaison on this dark, stormy night, that I had 'The Office' in tow and was proceeding to Santa Barbara. She acknowledged my call with relief, thanked me for my assistance and requested that I let them know when 'The Office' was safely tied up in harbour.

I called the fisherman whose boat was being tossed around behind us as we both shouldered the high seas that were hitting us abeam. He said he was OK, relieved to be out of there! I put AVTA on autopilot, patted her wheel affectionately and let out a big sigh of relief. I looked over at Rob who was wet and cold. We leaned over and 'high-fived' each other then I suggested he get into some warmer clothes. We were both coming down from the adrenaline high that had been keeping us going all night.

About 01:30 the wind seemed to lessen and the seas smoothed out and although they were still quite high, at least they were no longer so vicious.

Rob pulled out his harmonica, played a couple of blues tunes and then asked if he could catch some sleep. He crawled into the bunk, pulled the blanket over him and slept for over an hour. When he awoke I slept for about forty-five minutes and felt a little better.

Looking behind we could see the faint outline of 'The Office' as she rolled along behind us with the tow rope slackening and tightening. The land was getting closer both on the radar and visually as the lights of Santa Barbara became clearer.

The last time I had entered this narrow and winding harbour entrance was four months previously and I had never done it at night. I studied and re-studied my large-scale chart. Ten minutes before we reached the end of Stearn's Wharf, I wrapped up warm, left the cabin and climbed the steps to the fly-bridge. In the lee of the land the wind was light and the seas were calm - a noticeable difference from the witches' cauldron of just a few hours ago!

I radioed Santa Barbara Harbor Patrol on channel 12 to let them know that I would be towing in a disabled vessel. The patrolman informed me that the dredge was positioned at the harbor entrance but there were numerous buoys and I should just "follow the arrows". I thanked him, slowed the boat down and had Rob shorten up the towline. I switched off the autopilot and turned the wheel to the left.

Nothing happened..!

Well, not exactly nothing - there was a lot of clicking noise, the wheel spun lightly in my hand but the boat would not go in the direction I needed to! It was still dark and remembering the layout of the bay, I knew we would drift into the anchorage and eventually onto the beach (I would have set the anchor if necessary to prevent this).

Feeling a bit foolish, I called Santa Barbara Harbor Patrol again, told him of my predicament and requested assistance. He responded immediately and within five minutes came alongside.

I informed 'The Office' over the radio that we had no steering, he thought it quite apropos to the events of the night and it was obvious in his voice that he was happy to be in calm waters after his ordeal. We gathered in our towline and I maneuvered out of the way using just the twin throttles. Harbor Patrol hooked up to the Radon and slowly towed it through the very narrow winding entrance into the harbour. I followed him in, steering by using the two engines.

He secured 'The Office' alongside a commercial dock and I spun our boat against the guest dock and walked over to thank the Patrolman. He introduced himself as Brian and said he was glad of the opportunity to be of assistance - it had been a boring night!

I went around to meet the fisherman Luke to do the necessary paperwork. When he climbed out of his boat he looked me right in the eye, shook my hand hard and long and thanked me sincerely. As he was a member of Vessel Assist the twelve-hour job cost him nothing - had he not been a member the towing bill would have been over $1600.00! I retrieved my hook pole and staggered back to AVTA.

Dawn was just breaking, the gale had blown itself out, I climbed onto the fly-bridge, fired up the trusty Caterpillar diesels and jockeyed off the dock using my throttles. As I motored down the fairway I noticed that the red light on the autopilot panel was blinking. I pushed the engage button, the light stayed steady–I pushed it again and the light went out. I turned the wheel and it responded as if nothing had happened - I had my steering back!

I radioed the Coast Guard in Long Beach to let them know that

'The Office' was secure. They thanked me for my efforts on behalf of Luke and congratulated me on a job well done.

The next hour and a half were glorious. The sun came up, the visibility was endless, the sky was gorgeous, the seas behind us with a three to four foot swell. Rob played his harmonica as we surfed our way back to Ventura, occasionally yelling with delight when we caught a wave perfectly and rode it long with spray hissing over the foredeck. I called Joell on the VHF and it was obvious that it had been a sleepless night for her. She had kept the radio on and had heard the communications between the Coast Guard and me. She was anxiously awaiting my voice. It felt good to hear her and there is no doubt both she and Mum were relieved.

Half an hour before Ventura Harbour entrance I climbed onto the fly-bridge, switched off the autopilot and surfed through the entrance just for the sheer thrill of it. I felt good about saving Luke and his boat, I had learned a tremendous amount about AVTA, the area and my capabilities and I was hungry! David called me on the radio, sounded happy that all went well and invited us to Christy's for breakfast as soon as we tied up. As we motored to our slip, several boats in the harbour tooted their horns for us. We found out later that a lot of boats had been listening to our ordeal on the VHF radio!

Dave had spent a restless night himself, for having just moved his VHF radio was not yet hooked up at the house and he had no way of knowing what was going on. Over breakfast I related the events of the previous twelve hours and was a little concerned when I told him about the hole in the stern of the boat. He was just glad that we were unharmed - the boat could always be fixed.

Back to the dock at 08:45, all I wanted to do was turn in the paperwork and see my lovely wife and get some sleep. It was then I remembered that we had an in-harbour job scheduled for 0900 that morning - off we went...

THE SHARK AND THE MOSQUITOES

Once you leave the mansions of Naples, the southwest coast of Florida is mostly uninhabited everglades land laced with dozens of rivers and creeks and thousands of mangrove islands. Alligator Bay, Snake Bight and Jungle Bay are home to all types of creatures that swim, fly, crawl and slither through the moist, steamy, tropical swamps. Few people live there, mostly fishermen and rednecks, crackers and hermits. It's a beautiful, wild area but deadly and forbidding.

About halfway between the southern tip of Florida and the town of Naples on the Gulf Coast a river flows from the depths of the Everglades out to the Gulf of Mexico. It moves slowly, sluggishly and is a deep, dark brown from the silt that washes down with it. The entrance is protected by a small piece of land that juts out into the Gulf a few hundred feet. There is a navigation buoy to let you know you have arrived at a relatively safe place to anchor for the night.

We motored JoJo slowly up the river as dusk was beginning to fall. Having left Key Largo in the early morning we had enjoyed a lazy, hot sail northwest keeping a couple of miles offshore trying to avoid hundreds of crab traps. It was humid and muggy and we had stayed in the shade of the bimini top drinking lots of water. We had been in similar situations when we had explored uncharted rivers in western Panama a couple of years earlier aboard JoJo, our 32' Fisher catamaran.

There were no other boats, no sign of humans, just mangroves and palms and scrubby growth as far as we could see. A few stunted pines had somehow made a foothold and were determined to survive in this salty, eerie, silent place.

I throttled back when we were about half a mile up the river, the Shark River, gauging the current and looking for submerged trees.

The river wasn't very wide, maybe three hundred feet and a short way ahead it started to narrow and tree branches grew out threatening to tangle in the mast.

"Joie," I called and she turned from her position on the bow searching for obstructions.

"Come and take the wheel, love, I think I'll drop the hook here. There's room to swing and we're far enough from the banks so we shouldn't be bothered by any critters."

She grabbed the spokes of the small wooden ship's wheel and expertly held the boat in position while I lowered the anchor.

"Just let the current take us downstream. I'll see if the anchor holds."

Thirty seconds later the anchor dug itself into the mud of the river about fifteen feet down. I let out a little more rope and JoJo settled with a happy sigh as the river water gurgled around her bows. Walking back to the cockpit I was just about to say something to Joell when her mouth fell open, her eyes grew wide and she pointed behind me. I turned in time to see something large, long and serpentine disappear under the water.

"Oh my god, what was that?" I said.

"I don't know," replied Joell, "and I don't want to – let's go below and close up the boat."

The sun was beginning to fade and I swiped at a couple of angry mosquitoes. Joell went below and made sure all the bug screens were in place. I hurried into the cabin and closed the door quickly not wanting to let any flying, biting insects into our sanctum.

Switching on the electric fans I checked all the likely places that no-see-ums and mosquitoes could possibly get in. It was hot and stuffy but the little fans kept the air moving.

There is not much dusk in the tropics, nightfall comes quickly and by 7:00 pm we had eaten a light dinner and had converted the salon into a huge double berth, for we liked to be ready at a moment's notice when we were at anchor. Our cabin below was further away from the door and in case of an emergency I wanted to be able to get into the cockpit in two seconds.

A last look around and we snuggled under one light sheet, the fans blowing directly at us. It was calm and still outside and we lay in bed and watched a big, silver-white moon rise from the east over the swamps. The night was beautiful and serene, primeval and prehistoric. We drifted off to sleep...

Sometime in the early hours of the morning Joell nudged me.

"Wake up Jon, I just got bitten by a mosquito."

"Huh, wha'...swat it and go back to sleep," I grumbled, turning over.

A few minutes later, Joell shook me.

"I think there's a bunch of mosquitoes in here."

"Nah, no. The boat's all closed up. You're dreaming, go back to sleep. I'm tired..."

"No, I mean it, you've got to wake up and take a look," she insisted.

I opened my eyes and stared up at the overhead. The moon was still up and the cabin was bathed in its gentle light, enough so I could discern that the white overhead, the 'ceiling' was no longer white. It was black and it seemed to be moving. I rubbed my eyes and sure enough the entire overhead was undulating and throbbing and a buzzing sound was filling the cabin.

I looked over at Joell and was horrified to see blood on her arms and shoulders. Then there was a nasty buzzing in my ear and something bit me. I was now wide awake…

"Listen to me. Wrap the sheet around you and slowly climb over me. Go down to our cabin and close the door."

"What do you think happened?" she asked.

"Somehow the mosquitoes have found a way in and there are hundreds of them right above us on the overhead. They're getting louder and they might attack us. Get below now – I'm going to spray them…"

Joell is much more susceptible to bug bites than I am and already she had been bitten at least two dozen times. I had one or two bites but if they decided to attack us we would both be in very serious trouble.

Joell wrapped the blood-splattered sheet around her and stumbled below swatting at a few of the peskiest mosquitoes which had followed her. She closed the cabin door and I could hear her slapping at the ones that had flown in with her.

We had one can of bug spray but didn't like to use it as it is so toxic. This time I had no hesitation! I grabbed the can, aimed it at the mass of pulsing mosquitoes above me and pushed down on the button.

The reaction was instantaneous. Scores fell onto the bed dead and dying but many more got extremely pissed off and started flying around the cabin and at me. I emptied the can and killed dozens more.

All I had now was a fly swatter and in a few seconds it was matted with squashed mosquitoes. They bit me and buzzed in my ears. I yelled and swatted and danced around the small cabin. Somehow I managed to light a mosquito repellant and the sweet citronella fumes filled the salon.

I retreated below to our cabin, quickly opening the door and slamming it shut behind me. Joell was on the berth dabbing hydrocortisone cream on the bites she had sustained. She looked at me in horror, naked, bitten, bleeding, a mosquito-encrusted flyswatter in one hand, an empty can of bug spray in the other.

"I won," I yelled hysterically, "I got the little buggers – well, most of them!"

My adrenaline was pumping and I was panting heavily. A lone mosquito buzzed at me and with one deft flick of the swatter he buzzed no more.

Joell rubbed cream on me and I climbed into bed. I itched and scratched and couldn't sleep.

With daylight we went up to the salon and surveyed the carnage. There were literally hundreds if not thousands of dead mosquitoes, some squished, some dead from the spray, the rest from the mosquito repellant candle, its citrus fumes permeating the boat.

We swept them up, scraped them up, vacuumed them up and dumped them in the river. We wanted out of the Shark River before something else flew, crawled, swam or slithered aboard. Within five minute the anchor was up and we motored down the river and out into the brilliant blue of the Gulf.

And to this day we talk about what it was that we saw in the river that evening…

I discovered later that day that the mosquitoes had found a miniscule opening where the hot water heater vented. I sealed it but marveled that the carbon monoxide exhaled by us had frenetically driven them to find the only, tiny way in.

Also the Everglades are now home to thousands of giant non-native snakes and reptiles that have bred and multiplied over the past twenty years. Unthinking people who buy small snakes then set them loose when they grow too big, have caused massive damage to the fragile eco system that is the Everglades. There are huge Burmese pythons in there that have been captured and killed and revealed half-digested alligators in their stomachs! Was that what we had seen as we dropped the anchor that day? And they can easily slither onto a boat..!

KASHMIR ADVENTURES

Part 1

Into the foothills of the Himalayas

When I was a young boy growing up in London I used to read a weekly comic magazine called the 'Beano'. One of the serials was about a 'fearless white hunter' who roamed through an exotic country called Kashmir protecting the meek natives from tigers and lions. I had pulled out my atlas and discovered there really was such a place, in northern India in the foothills of the Himalayas. I looked forward to reading his exploits each week usually late at night in a tent I made in my bed with a torch to read by and a length of rubber hose as a breathing tube!

Twelve years later I was squashed into an ancient, wheezing bus, the only foreigner surrounded by smiling old Indian ladies in dazzling saris, young families with happy, boisterous kids and an assortment of chickens and goats, labouring up dangerous mountain passes on my way to Srinigar, the capital of Kashmir. One family had lit a charcoal fire at the back of the bus and were boiling eggs. An Indian man sang a melodious song and others clapped and sang along. The air was pungent with the exotic smells of Asia – curry, turmeric, jasmine, cardamom, sweat...

The bus was suddenly enveloped by dark as we squeezed into a narrow rock tunnel, low, dank, dripping with water. I sat by the window seeing nothing, thinking how I came to be here living a childhood fantasy.

A few days before, my friends Pat and Dave had decided to leave Delhi and make their way north to a place we had heard about from hippies as we traveled along parts of the fabled Old Silk Road.

There was a large lake in Kashmir surrounded by mountains where you could rent a beautiful houseboat and be waited on by servants for just a few dollars a week. I had to stay in Delhi by myself waiting for money to be sent to the American Express office and now that it had arrived and I had a couple of hundred dollars in my pocket, I was on my way up the foothills of the Himalayas to join them.

The dark seemed to go on and on and I realized we were inside the Kashmir Valley Tunnel which burrowed more than a mile through the foothills. We emerged into blinding sunlight and I peered down at a precipitous drop just inches from where the bus clung to the road. It is four hundred grueling, hot, scary miles from Delhi to Srinigar and the previous night we had stopped in Jammu to sleep. I didn't know it at the time but I would be spending a lot more time in Jammu on the way back and would have a life-altering experience there.

As the sun started to set and bathed the surrounding Himalaya Mountains in a purple glow we spluttered into the old bus station in Srinigar. The bus seemed to sigh with relief as people clambered down from the roof and threw bags and assorted livestock onto the road. I jumped out of the bus cheerily waving goodbye to the people I had spent the last two days with.

Pat was waiting for me and we walked a mile or so toward the lake. Suddenly there it was, this vast body of water, serene and glistening in the sunset surrounded by majestic, shimmering mountains, lined with magnificent wooden houseboats of all sizes. Small canoes were crisscrossing the lake and many fires were being lit as the sun sank lower. I marveled at this magic place as Pat led me up the gangplank onto a 60 foot teak floating palace. This was to be my home for the next three weeks at the affordable price of one dollar a day per person, including meals!

I met the others who would be living here including a languorous Dutch girl named Anneke. After being shown my bed I wandered around the boat intrigued by the gorgeous carvings and wall hangings. Soon I was called onto the aft deck and there was a large table piled high with naan and dishes of curries and vegetables. I met our servant family who lived on a small, plain houseboat tied to the back of ours.

And then we ate and ate, sang songs, smoked fine Kashmiri kif, drank bad wine and told stories and tales of far off places and the adventures we had. Other travelers from many different countries wandered over to our floating palace and soon there were two or three dozen long-haired hippies playing guitars, beating drums, making music through the Himalayan night. Sometimes when you're having an adventure you don't realize it at the time, unless it's uncomfortable or dangerous. But even though we were safe on the boat, being taken care of, adventure was waiting; in fact being on Dal Lake was an adventure in itself!

The next afternoon Anneke suggested we borrow a small canoe from our servant family and paddle out into the middle of the lake to watch the sun set behind the mountains. I readily agreed and after providing ourselves with some food and water I paddled away and eventually let the canoe drift. Anekke lay in the canoe next to me with a curious smile on her face. She reached into her pocket and pulled out two little purple pills. We each ate one and the next twelve hours were magical beyond belief as we floated on the lake and in our minds. The deep magenta of the mountains as the sun set was intensified, the water lapping at the canoe made music and we drifted off into a star-filled night...

We enjoyed Srinigar together for the next three weeks. We explored the markets and tried different foods. We climbed the hills and were invited into homes to drink chai. I met a merchant who showed me beautiful Kashmiri sheepskin coats, delicate wood carvings and exquisite jewelry. We struck a deal and I agreed to buy $5000 worth of Kashmiri handicrafts from him when I returned to America. But it was not to be. Amongst all this beauty and graciousness there were ominous rumblings of war…

Occasionally as the bus had made its way up the mountain road we had been forced to stop and wait for a caravan of glistening tanks and rockets on giant transporters coming from somewhere in China, heading for the India/Pakistan border. In Pakistan several weeks earlier there had been a fervour of anger with India over the long-disputed Kashmir territory. Many cars had bumper stickers that read 'Crush India'. There was talk of war but no one in India gave it much credence.

Now it seemed more real, there was word coming in that Pakistani politicians were whipping people into a frenzy, that war was inevitable. America was supplying Pakistan with old tanks and guns and was supporting their cause. In India all seemed calm although the weapons I saw in the mountains were new, menacing and apparently Chinese made. The peace of the last few nights had occasionally been shattered by a distant 'crump' as an artillery shell found a target.

There was a small community of western hippies living on the lake and we had a big dinner to discuss what to do. A few said they were going far south to Goa on the coast, some said they would head to Nepal and the general consensus was that Kashmir would not be the best place to hang out if war came.

The next day Anneke left heading for Nepal. I had decided to travel far south to Goa where there was a large hippie community living on the beach under the palm trees next to the sea. Everyone was splitting up, some deciding to head back west to Afghanistan before the India/Pakistan border closed. We had a large farewell meal on the boat, rice, eggs, naan, curries and vegetables.

The following morning I headed to the bus station alone and bought a ticket for the first bus down the mountains to New Delhi via Jammu.

I had felt a little queasy when I woke up that morning and as the bus lurched down the mountains, the engine whining in protest as it was kept in a low gear, my queasiness grew into severe stomach pain and I broke out in a sweat. I staggered up to the driver and motioned him to pull over. He protested but agreed. I disappeared into the bushes and quickly got rid of the huge meal from the night before.

But I felt very weak and disoriented. An hour later I made the driver stop again and this time there was blood in my movement. Somehow I made it back to the bus, people were muttering about how I was wasting time making the bus stop. But I didn't hear them for long because, covered in sweat and shaking, I passed out...

Part 2

The Hospital from Hell

I felt someone pulling at me and opened my eyes. There were two young Indian men peering down at me, both showing genuine concern on their faces. One thing I had noticed about Indian people – they were usually gracious, curious and above all, kind. They said I had been unconscious for several hours and we were now in the town of Jammu. I tried to stand but my legs wouldn't support me. They each put one of my arms over their shoulders and helped me off the bus. I was sweating and in intense pain, everything was blurry. Grabbing my backpack they hustled me into an old Hindi taxi.

"We will take you to the hospital, very, very quickly," said one in the melodic, sing-song way the native Indian speaks English.

All I could do was nod in agreement. Belching blue smoke, the ancient taxi lurched off down narrow, winding streets, the driver constantly beeping his horn to shoo cows and pedestrians out of the road. Fifteen minutes later we braked in front of a long, rambling stone structure. One of my saviours ran inside and a few minutes later came back with two stretcher bearers. I was gently lifted onto the canvas stretcher, my pack was placed at my feet and I was hurried inside, into another century, another world, another reality…

The hospital looked (and smelled) like it probably had a hundred and fifty years ago when it had been built by the British Empire. The walls had once been white although they were now grimy and dirty from years of neglect. The corridors were long and low and it seemed like I was carried along for ages, down hallways and passageways, up stairs, down stairs, through countless doors in the murky light.

Enquiring faces peered down at me, some smiling, some grave. As I lay panting and sweating it all seemed surrealistic and unreal. There was a pervasive smell in the air as of cooking meat but I found out later it was the funeral pyres of those who had died in the hospital – for the next week I smelled burning human flesh all day and all night. Many people died there…

At last I was carried into a small room and the stretcher was put down on the floor. One of the young men who had brought me here from the bus looked down at me, smiled and said a doctor would be here soon. He said his name was Adi and he would come back to see me. Then he was gone and I was left alone on a stretcher on the floor alternating between chills and fever, my stomach feeling like a fire pit.

I don't know how long I lay there but eventually a man in a grubby white coat came in and asked for my passport. He wrote on a form and told someone out of sight to please bring me a cup of tea!

He asked me some questions, felt around my stomach and gravely informed me that I had dysentery, probably amoebic dysentery and I would have to stay in the hospital for a while.

Before I could get my tea, which I couldn't have kept down anyway, the stretcher was picked up and I began another 'Alice in Wonderland' journey up and down stairs and along corridors and hallways, the crying sounds of people in pain, the smell of those outside burning. The stretcher would tip as I was carried up stairs and then tip the other way as we went down. I was nauseous, cold, hot, almost delirious with the turmoil going on in my intestines.

And always the faces peering down at me as we moved past, word obviously having spread about the foreign traveler being admitted to this hellish place. Looks of encouragement with bright smiles, looks of concern with grave countenances, moved in and out of my field of vision, blurred and indistinct.

Finally I was carried into a small ward with a few beds. Only one of them was occupied and I was gently placed on a rickety white bed frame and the stretcher pulled out from under me. A nurse came in and wiped the sweat from my face. Then she fussed around with a needle and inserted a drip into my arm. This was a painful procedure as she wasn't very good at it!

Over the next few hours I fell in and out of consciousness. There was always someone standing over me when I would open my eyes – a nurse, a helper but mostly patients in ragged clothes just staring at me, curiosity and concern on their faces. My hair was long and tangled, my beard was thick – perhaps I looked like a western Sikh to them!

My backpack lay at the foot of my bed and I was worried that it would be stolen but that never happened. Apparently there was a code of honour here that you don't rob from someone who is in the same wretched state you are...

I had nightmares and suffered intense pain the first night, somehow managing to get up with the help of whoever was standing next to my bed, not noticing who they were, in order to go to the toilet. Needless to say, here as in most of India flushing toilets were unheard of. A hole in the floor and a pitcher of water to clean yourself. Flies, excrement, filth.

In the morning a nervous nurse brought me a cup of sweet tea. I smiled a weak thank you to her and she scurried off. I took a sip and instantly threw up. It seemed I could keep nothing down. The doctor finally came in, his badge proclaiming him to be Dr. A. Gupta, very professional and doctor-like, full of his own importance as an educated man surrounded by poor, ignorant peasants.

"Well, well, well," he chirped. "Yes, yes, you have the dysentery very, very bad. You are totally dehydrated and I think it will be quite some time before you can eat anything, yes."

"How long must I be here?" I croaked, my dry throat rasping.

"Well, well, that is very difficult to say. You are very weak and must let your body gain strength and balance. It could be days, it could be weeks. But we will make sure you are very comfortable here in our fine hospital!"

I laughed inwardly and thanked him for his concern and care.

"That is no problem, I will keep you on the IV drip and you must drink tea as much as you are able."

"How much will this cost me a day?" I asked.

My money was running low and I had no way of having more wired to me here in this remote town. In fact, no one knew I was here, not my friends who were themselves traveling south or east, nor anyone outside of India. I was totally alone with no way to communicate my situation.

"Oh, no, no, no, sir. There is no charge for medical assistance in India – we have a perfect health system supported by our government. Please do not concern yourself at all about the cost," he answered.

The next two days the pain in my gut grew worse and worse. I had a book on Hatha Yoga that I had been studying for the past few weeks. I remembered to focus all my energy to the part of my body that was hurting, willing it to get better. I was losing weight rapidly, a combination of the dehydration and not being able to eat anything. I felt weak and confused.

On the third day I woke from a fitful, sweat-filled sleep and the pain was so intense it felt like a burning sun in my stomach. I rolled and flopped on the bed and yanked the I.V. out of my arm. The pain grew worse, it was like a giant ball of flame, everything became yellow, orange, deep red...The physical agony was so intense and all-pervasive that something 'snapped' and my body crossed into another place where the pain became pleasure.

Perhaps it was the only way my body and conscious mind could handle it, could get through this; crossing over a threshold of pain and transmuting it into an intense, almost pleasurable sensation.

And then suddenly, miraculously, the feeling stopped. It literally went away and I felt a lightness in my mind and in my body. And there was a light around me as well, calling to me, pulling me up. I opened my eyes and looked down on my body in the rumpled hospital bed. I heard and saw the doctor come running in and quickly examining me.

"Goodness gracious me, he has stopped breathing," he called to the nurse as several people came rushing over.

44

I looked down on this unfolding drama with a tranquility and calm I had never known before. And I felt myself being drawn toward a light, a peaceful, all-surrounding light that beckoned me away from here. The doctor was pushing on my chest trying to get me to breathe again.

And initially I resisted. I felt I had a choice – to start breathing and return to the world or to move toward the welcoming light. But I knew it wasn't my time to pass over and I almost reluctantly moved back into the body lying on the bed and started to take deep breaths.

"Ah, good, very good," said Dr. Gupta. "I have brought him back. Now see, he is breathing again and it was only a few seconds, so he will be fine, yes, yes."

It had seemed timeless to me but apparently it was only a few seconds! There were lots of people, both staff and patients crammed around my bed now all smiling and clucking away at my miraculous rescue from death. Dr. Gupta's reputation probably grew immensely at that moment as I'm sure that many times his patients did not recover in that primitive, unsanitary hospital.

I felt better, the pain in my intestines was subsiding. A nurse wiped the sweat from my head and I tried to explain to Dr. Gupta that I had looked down on my body at him working on me.

"Ah," he chuckled. "So you are now another incarnation, are you?"

I don't know if he believed me. I wasn't sure what to believe either but I knew something profound had happened. (Many months later I read a book by noted NDE expert Elizabeth Kubler-Ross and wrote her a letter explaining what had happened to me. She wrote back agreeing that I had experienced a near-death experience).

This was a life-altering event and it has stayed with me always. Perhaps it is part of the reason I choose such an adventurous life, sailing the oceans, taking risks. Perhaps it is because I believe there is something wonderful after death, that I don't fear it?

I drank a cup of sweet tea and kept it down. I fell asleep, a long, untroubled, painless sleep. I woke to find Adi, the young man who had brought me to the hospital days before sitting by my bed holding my hand.

"Ah, Jon, I am so happy to see you recovering," he said.

"Adi, how long have you been here?"

"Oh, Jon, I have come here every day and sat beside you when you were in pain and you did not know what was happening around you. I have been here at different times to make sure you are alright."

"I didn't know, I was really out of my mind, I didn't know who was here or if anyone was here. Thank you, thank you so much."

He smiled and his head bobbed from side to side.

"Oh no, you would have done the same for me if I was sick and alone in your country, yes?"

"Yes," I replied, "of course I would."

And this was another life-altering realization for me – that there are good, genuinely good people in the world who help others for nothing in return, just because it is the right thing to do.

The next day I ate some naan and a little rice. I was able to sleep for several hours at a time without having to rush to the toilet. Then a little more rice and soup. I could walk around, albeit unsteadily with Adi walking next to me, ready to catch me.

I looked in a mirror and couldn't believe the gaunt, drawn, thin face looking back was me. I was skin and bones and weighed less than 120 lbs! There wasn't an ounce of fat on me – my body had used it all to survive the past week.

Part 3

Trapped at the border

Now that I could walk and keep a little food and liquid in me, I determined to get out of Jammu as quickly as I could. Adi told me that there would definitely be war, Pakistan would likely attack India any day. If that happened the border would be closed and there would be no chance of heading back to the States for treatment for a long time. I knew that in my present condition I needed more help and medical attention than I could get in India and had no alternative but to head west. I met with Dr. Gupta and he urged me to stay and get my strength back.

"No," I told him. "I must leave today and get to the border at Lahore before it is closed otherwise I could be stuck in India for months."

"But, no," he insisted. "You are still weak and sick. You could have a relapse and die."

"Then I'll take my chances. I'll sign the release form but I must leave now."

With Adi at my side I stumbled back to my ward, took a quick shower under a thin trickle of cold water and said goodbye to the staff and the patients who I had met. A nurse came in with a release form and I signed it, agreeing that I was leaving against the doctor's orders.

Adi carried my pack through the winding hallways out to a waiting taxi. He helped me in the back and climbed in the front seat. We rattled through the streets to the bus station. Adi found the next bus to Amritsar and tearfully we said goodbye. The taxi driver took a photo of us together and then with one last hug he helped me aboard, tossed in my pack and the bus rattled out of town, Adi waving goodbye until he was lost to sight.

It's only 75 miles as the crow flies from Jammu to Amritsar but it took ten hours down tortuous, twisting roads, stopping at little villages to load and unload passengers and livestock. I felt weak but exhilarated, glad to be out of the hospital from hell, hoping to get to the border before it was closed. We bumped and jostled into Amritsar the Golden City of the Sikhs at dusk. As I staggered down from the bus I was surrounded by a dozen ragged urchins, each assuring me they represented "the best hotel, very cheap, very clean". Also, "the best young virgins, very cheap, very clean!"

I chose one little boy to lead me to a hotel and after a few minutes' walk we entered a courtyard. I looked at the small room, paid a few rupees and lay down on the tattered blanket. After sleeping for a couple of hours I ventured out to find food. This was a sacred town renowned for the famous Golden Temple, the holiest shrine of the Sikhs. I walked a little way to a small restaurant where I was viewed suspiciously. I sat down and ordered naan bread and soup. Soon I was surrounded by a gang of young beggars demanding money. I quickly ate my food, threw a few rupees on the street and left as fast as I could while they scrambled to pick up the coins.

I slept a few more hours then forgoing my chance to see the Temple I got the first bus heading west down the Grand Trunk Road. It's less than twenty miles from Amritsar to the outskirts of Lahore, the first city in Pakistan. I talked to people on the bus who told me that Pakistan had lobbed more shells into India a couple of nights ago.

They feared war would break out any day, perhaps any hour. No one knew if the border would still be open.

The bus stopped at the border post on the Indian side, we all got out, the bus picked up a few passengers and then slowly trundled back toward Amritsar. Next to the road was a small collection of huts and some tables outside in the stifling heat, under green, camouflaged army tents. A dozen severe-looking Sikhs in army uniforms sat behind the tables and one waved me over.

He looked me up and down and apparently didn't like what he saw. I didn't blame him. My hair was long and wild, my beard was matted and straggly, I was emaciated and pale, my clothes hung off me and I didn't smell that great!

"Is the border still open, sir?" I asked respectfully.

"Passport and border pass," he barked at me.

I gave him my passport but didn't know what he meant by 'border pass'.

"What border pass, sir?"

"The paper you were given when you entered India- that border pass. Where is it?" he responded curtly.

I looked through my wallet, my passport, turned everything out of my pack.

"I don't have it, sir – I must have lost it when I was in hospital."

"Then you will have to go back to Delhi and try to get another one, then come back here," he said, disinterestedly.

"But that will take days and the border could be closed. I'm sick,

49

I've been in hospital in Jammu and I must get home for medical attention," I beseeched.

"NO – you cannot cross the border without your pass, now go away." And I was dismissed.

I moved outside, angry at this rude man, scared that I wouldn't be able to get out of India for months. I sat down near the tents and stared into space. What could I do? Sneaking across was out of the question. There was a 'no-man's land' about a quarter mile wide and each side was covered by soldiers with machine guns.

At night there were giant spotlights which now sat darkened along the border. I rested in the shade of a huge banyan tree trying to come up with a plan. Could I forge a border pass? Could I hide in the back of a vehicle? Could I bribe someone? This seemed the most likely choice and I was counting my little money when a shadow loomed over me.

It was an army officer, another Sikh, his beard neatly plaited, his hair (which traditionally had never been cut) looped inside his scarlet turban. He wore a crisp uniform and carried a swagger stick under his arm, like British officers of old. His olive skin glistened in the broiling sun.

"What is your problem, sir?" he asked kindly.

I explained what had happened and how I was dismissed rudely and told to return to Delhi. He looked over my passport, put it in his pocket and told me to wait there. He strode off purposefully toward the largest hut. I was alarmed because he had my passport without which I was really stuck.

Half an hour later, he came back and ordered me to follow him. We walked into the hut where a clerk stamped my passport. Then two Indian soldiers came in and they each grabbed one of my arms in a vice-like grip. A third soldier took my backpack.

Outside four more soldiers were lined up with rifles pointed at me. I didn't know what was happening but for a second thought I was going to be shot right there! Then two of the soldiers moved in front of me and two took positions behind. With my arms pinned to my side the seven soldiers marched this hippy a quarter of a mile down the road to where a red-and-white striped barrier defined the border between the soon-to-be-warring nations of India and Pakistan.

With their rifles still aimed at me the four soldiers moved back and the two holding my arms let go. I was handed my backpack and told to wait until the barrier was raised and then walk across. I turned around and looked back down the road. Standing afar was the kind Sikh officer who had arranged my escort to the border. I stood to attention and gave him a rigid salute. He returned the salute, smiled and went into his hut...

I turned at the sound of marching boots coming from the Pakistani side. Six soldiers were hurrying toward the barrier, bayonets on their rifles pointed at me. The gate was raised and I walked over, my pack on my back, my hands in the air. The same formation, two in front, one on either side, two behind, frog marched me into Pakistan. Preliminaries at the border, inspection and stamping of my passport and then I was shown into a small hut where a short, self-important army officer sat behind a big desk.

"So, you have been in Jammu for a while – what armaments did you see, how many soldiers, what is their attitude, do they have many guns, how many trucks, how many tanks, missiles?"

I was shocked. It seems the reason the Pakistanis allowed me across the border was to interrogate me about their enemy. I had grown to like the Indian people very much – their kindness and generosity had helped me many times. I had experienced problems traveling through Pakistan on the way east. And their war fever and rage had alarmed me all those weeks ago.

"Sir," I replied, "I appreciate your helping me to get across the border but I spent my time in Jammu in a hospital. I have no idea what the state of the Indian army is there. And I left at night, so did not see any artillery or guns."

This was not true but I wasn't going to tell him that the Indians had lots of brand new, Chinese made weaponry aimed right at Lahore. Let them get their own spies…

He drummed his fingers on the table and scowled at me. I didn't know if he would order me back across the border but he told me brusquely to get out and leave Lahore now. I was only too happy to do that, grabbed my pack and walked as quickly as I could toward the town. I flagged down a rickshaw and headed right to the bus station.

There I boarded a bus for Peshawar, the town on the Pakistan/Afghan border. I couldn't wait to get out of Pakistan, back to my friend Abdullah and his family in Herat. As the bus finally filled with passengers and chickens and lurched off west I contemplated the thousands of miles ahead of me. But that is another story…

LOST SAILOR

About a day's sail east of the Rio Dulce River in Guatemala, close to Isla Roatan is the mainland city of La Ceiba in Honduras. In 1998 it had suffered terribly from Hurricane Mitch when torrential rains loosened mountainsides and buried thousands of people.

The town itself is the third largest in Honduras, a mixture of Spanish colonial and almost-modern. There are wonderful old plazas, busy commercial areas, fruit markets and even a couple of internet cafes. I created the web site for Ladyhawke Charters over a two-month period here. We liked La Ceiba, we never felt in any danger, the people were friendly and it was very cheap! For cruising sailors, the Marina Lagoon and the nearby La Ceiba Boatyard offered many services.

A few hundred yards up a meandering river in the dense jungle, a young German couple had spent the previous three years carving out and building a small marina, complete with swimming pool, an unfinished fabricating shop and about twenty slips. We tied Ladyhawke alongside, at 64 feet she was by far the largest yacht there. Lush trees made a canopy overhead, there were carefully tended paths through the jungle, little gardens of tropical plants and flowers, birds shrilling in the treetops.

Downtown La Ceiba was a one-dollar, twenty-minute taxi ride away but sometimes we had to walk a mile or two to find a taxi. It was stifling hot and very humid in July but we had work to do to get the yacht ready for our planned charter business in Panama. We settled in for a couple of months, got to know the town and started to varnish and paint. We also spent a lot of time in the swimming pool, drinking cold beer and chatting with other cruisers!

The weather is fairly unsettled during the summer and in hurricane season a huge storm may power up the coast, wreaking havoc and destruction. We knew we had to leave La Ceiba by mid-August in order to make the 200-mile beat to the eastern tip of Honduras then turn south toward Panama and out of the normal path of hurricanes.

We'd been there about a month and our Schipperke 'Sailor', well known in the cruising community was always leashed when off the boat. On one sweltering, musty day, there was an electricity in the air. Something was happening with the weather, probably some heavy rain. It gets dark quickly in the tropics and about 7:00 p.m., just after dusk, there was a crash of thunder and a huge streak of lightning. You could feel the energy in the air, smell the rain and suddenly it was there cascading down out of the dark, ominous clouds. As the second lightning bolt sizzled across the sky and the thunder roared closer, Sailor scrambled up the companionway steps, dashed across the cockpit, leaped onto the dock and ran, all in a matter of seconds...

I yelled to Joell, she yelled back, the rain came down in sheets, the thunder rumbled, the lightning lit up the jungle and our little friend Sailor was gone.

I threw my waterproof on and grabbed a flashlight, jumped off the boat yelling for Sailor at the top of my voice. Joell was there seconds later calling for Sailor. But the thunder was so loud and the sound of the rain hitting on a thousand branches swallowed our cries.

I took off toward the swimming pool and buildings, calling out for Sailor, shining my flashlight everywhere. Joell ran down the docks screaming his name. The ground rapidly became muddy and large puddles appeared everywhere. Within twenty minutes the deluge had created small lakes and rivers. The vivid lightning flashes threw grotesque shadows everywhere and then it became pitch black again.

I ran out of the marina, down the road toward town, calling his name, crying with the fear that I'd never see him again. He could be anywhere, a local could have grabbed him (they were enchanted by the little black 'Lobito'), he could have been attacked by a gang of starving feral dogs, he could have fallen in the river. I dashed back to the marina, sloshing through the mud, hardly able to see as the rain continued its heavy, blinding onslaught.

The owners' German shepherd came loping up to me, seemingly anxious to help look for his little friend. I literally bumped into Joell who also had no luck. We were both hoarse from yelling "Sailor" and were both crying at the thought of what could have happened to him. We were drenched and sweating, feet cut from the rocks and stones, legs and arms slashed by jungle thorns and low branches. We made our way back to the boat, sad and dejected.

We had found Sailor through the International Schipperke Rescue in Ft. Lauderdale eighteen months earlier. He had been a stray and we knew that given the chance, he would run off and not come back. We doubted we'd see our little shipmate again…

I walked around the dark, steamy marina, trying to put myself into his mind.

"Where would a scared animal go when the rains made the ground difficult to walk, especially one with short legs?" I asked myself.

"More than likely to higher ground, out of a need to survive," was my answer.

But where around here? The unfinished fabricating shop had a rough concrete stairway running up to the roof with rebar sticking up, waiting for the walls of the second storey. It was open to the elements, with bags of covered concrete and lumber lying around.

I rushed over there, branches slapping my face, eyes like slits against the pounding rain. I took the stairs two at a time, stumbled onto the open roof and there as I aimed the barely functioning flashlight, huddled in a corner, shaking and miserable, eyes wide with fear was a little black bundle of soaking fur.

I picked him up, feeling joyful and grateful and carefully made my way down the stairs and sprinted back to the boat, yelling to Joell all the way. We dried him, fed him, calmed him down and each drank a large glass of rum!

And then as suddenly as it started, the rain stopped, the storm moved on and the stars came out blinking in the dark, tropical night. Everything was dripping, waterfalls and streams snaked down the hillside and we had our Sailor back.

TRUCK DRIVING SCHOOL

Having spent several months starting, growing and finally selling our Natural Health Magazine in Juno Beach, Florida in 2002 we felt the need for a complete change in our lives. Arranging for our catamaran 'JoJo' to be stored ashore inland, we spent a few days chugging up the Intracoastal Waterway and across Lake Okeechobee and were hauled out at Glades Boat storage in the middle of Florida where she would be landlocked for over a year.

Our classic Jaguar XJ6 had blown its engine up a few weeks earlier, so after renting a car we drove back to pick up the Bugatti and stored her under a tarp next to the boat. Packing two bags, we boarded a Greyhound bus in La Belle and headed to Spartanburg, S.C. to begin our training as a long-distance truck driving team...

The major national transport companies were always desperate to find drivers as the turnover in their industry is nearly one hundred percent. C.R. England, Inc., a large trucking conglomerate were happy to have us go through their driving school although they charged a lot for the privilege! The weather had changed from the sultry heat of Florida to cold and rain within a few hundred miles.

We arrived at the rather bleak school situated a few miles from the town of Spartanburg in the middle of nowhere. After checking in, we were shown a room of our own which was furnished with a bed, nothing more. The majority of students were single, poor men from rural America – they slept in small dormitories, six to a room.

There were about twenty-five of us in our class, Joell and I standing out as a middle-aged, relatively well-educated couple. The first two days were in a classroom filling out forms, being divided into smaller groups and meeting our instructors. They were there not only to instruct us how to drive a big rig, but also in what the company expected of us. The temperature dropped, it snowed, we both developed colds and Joell spent her 50th birthday sniffling in a classroom.

There was no restaurant at the school, just coffee and soda machines along with a large, communal refrigerator. Every day at about 5:00 in the afternoon, those who wanted to could board the school's yellow bus and get dropped off at a small shopping centre near the town. There were some fast food restaurants and a small grocery store where we stocked up with the healthiest food we could find.

Most of the students were initially a bit wary of Joell and I, they had not met anyone like us before. One of the young black guys who we christened 'New York' had never been out of that city and had never walked in mud or seen fields of trees. 'Mississippi', a thin, gangly twenty-year old was in awe of Joell and refused to call her anything but 'Mizz White' – he told us his Mama would slap him if he didn't show respect for women. But there were some at the school who had missed that life lesson…

The fourth day we were there, having spent hours getting familiar with the ten-speed transmissions of the training trucks, Joell and I boarded the school bus to go to town. It was packed as always. After having been dropped off and completing some small shopping, we drifted back to the pickup spot and waited with about forty others for the ride 'home'.

When the bus pulled up a bunch of rowdy black guys pushed aboard and headed to the back seats, their chosen domain. Joell and I sat toward the front. There were three single white women, two other couples and about twenty white men.

As we trundled back towards the school, the dozen or so black guys in the back were talking loudly and getting rowdier. Their voices were excited, they were good-naturedly yelling back and forth to each other, slapping high fives. In the front we minded our own business, talked softly to each other and tried to stay warm. The yelling in the back started to get raunchy, shouting demeaning remarks about women. As their taunting became more lurid and detailed I felt a knot tightening in my stomach.

I didn't show it and tried to ignore what was being joked about in the back. The other women were also getting uncomfortable and looking around I saw some guys staring out the window trying to ignore the rising tension.

After another couple of minutes I couldn't take the language and humiliation any longer. With Joell grabbing my arm to keep me down I stood up in my seat and turned around to face them. There were about ten black men, most of them much bigger and definitely meaner than me.

"Gentlemen," I called. "Gentlemen," louder.

All of a sudden all eyes were on me. The driver, a small, older man slowed the bus down and looked at me in his mirror. Joell went pale. The noise slowly subsided as ten angry black faces stared at me in disbelief. The whole bus went quiet. My knees went weak but I had committed myself.

"Gentlemen, please - there are ladies on this bus. Keep your voices down and your inappropriate comments to yourself…"

I turned around and sat back down figuring I was about to be dead. Joell couldn't believe what I had done; neither could I and neither could the rest of the bus, especially the big black guys in the back. For the rest of the drive they were quiet, muttering amongst themselves – I could sense them looking at me.

When we pulled up to the school, Joell and I tried to get off the bus quickly but a group of students formed a protective barrier and told me I had done the right thing and they would fight with me if the situation deteriorated to that.

We stepped down and started to head indoors. The biggest black man yelled out to me to wait. I turned around to face him as Joell pulled at my arm to hurry me inside. He jumped down from the bus followed by his friends and they all walked right up to me. I was scared, I was very scared....

Everyone went quiet, he raised his right hand and I flinched expecting to see a big fist come right at me. Instead he put his hand out to shake mine. He looked humble and apologized for being out of line. I gripped his hand and looked right into his eyes, accepted his apology and slowly released my sphincter muscle.

We walked into the building together, his friends following, looking contrite. He respected my standing up for my wife and promised to "be a gentleman" around us. Not only was he true to his word but I gained a huge measure of respect and was considered a 'brother' from then on. We became friends, they invited us to eat with them and for the next three weeks Joell and I were honorary black brothers. Over coffee the next day we found out that the leader, Deshawn had just been released from jail and was trying to go straight!

We finished the two weeks of school, Joell at the top of our class! We were flown out to company headquarters in Salt Lake City, passed some more tests then spent an incredible month driving around the country with our young, black training driver Derek, before we leased our own gleaming red truck and took to the open road...

HURRICANE – Sail Away, Sail Away!!

We left the marina in La Ceiba, Honduras on August 2, 2004 after a humid, buggy month working hard on the boat. A gentle three-hour motor took us back to the lovely Cochinos Cays where we spent a week snorkeling, resting and visiting friends. One morning, a gleaming 100' stinkpot (powerboat) steamed in and dropped its anchor right in front of us. Immediately they winched a noisy jet ski over the side, turned on their loud generator and filled the quiet bay with raucous music...time to go.

Luckily the weather forecast was for diminishing winds so we headed east into the trade winds, sailing toward a small reef nearly two hundred miles away. It was an uneventful passage, took about thirty-seven hours but we arrived at night and it was pitch black. With no radar aboard, I carefully used the GPS and depth sounder to inch close under the limited protection of the low reef. We dropped the anchor and slept for ten hours.

What a sight greeted us the next morning – the Vivarillo Cays consist of three small, low-lying, palm-covered islets joined by a mile-long, crescent shaped reef in the middle of the ocean! We had anchored a mere hundred yards off the reef and the seas were crashing over it. I dropped the dinghy and attached the motor and fuel tank; Sailor our Schipperke leaped aboard, anxious to relieve himself on land!

I motored to the nearest little island with Sailor hoarsely barking at the dozens of curious birds circling low over us. As we neared the island I could see a funky little fishermen's camp and someone was waving us over. I went ashore and met Arnold, Lydia, their boy Daniel and their friend, Ryan O'Neal(!). Sailor found a playmate with their dog and I marveled at the Robinson Crusoe-like camp where this family spent two months at a time fishing and diving.

I helped Arnold fix his generator and he gave us fourteen large lobsters, five huge conchs and a monstrous crab – we ate well that night and had a freezer full of meals for the future...

Two nights later, with squalls producing jagged lightning, loud thunder and heavy winds, Joell woke at 2:30 a.m. and immediately roused me.

"We're dragging, I think," she said urgently.

I leaped into the cockpit and the lightning flashes showed that we had moved about three hundred yards and were facing in the opposite direction. As there were numerous reefs around us it would be imprudent to motor around to find a good spot to reset the anchor. We had planned to leave that morning for Isla Providencia, almost two hundred miles southeast on our way to Panama.

"Let's go now," I suggested.

Joell agreed and much to Sailors' dismay I hurriedly hauled the dinghy on board and lashed it down. Joell ran around below, securing everything she could. At 3:30 a.m. using our electronic charts on the computer we cautiously headed out to sea, around the island. The waves were large and confused, the wind was strangely blowing from the west and we were tossed around uncomfortably in our large, stable 64' trimaran.

About fifteen minutes out, the autopilot stopped working – I switched to manual and found that we had no steering! Turning the large wheel port or starboard had no effect. In the dark night, with lightning, thunder and five-foot seas I scrambled down to the small aft compartment where the steering quadrant is housed.

Shining a torch on the mechanism, the problem was apparent and fixable, but it would be tricky and take a little time. With Joell watching our position I climbed back up and took the inspection cover off the transom.

Now the waves were crashing over me and entering the generator room threatening to flood it. The next twenty minutes were a nightmare as I threaded a fitting back on and attempted to line up a small pin and its hole with the heavy rudder doing its best to thwart my attempts. In the process I got a deep, jagged cut and nasty bruise on a finger but eventually put it all together. One of the waves knocked our computer's flat monitor over in the main cabin and the computer suddenly locked up.

We had drifted away from the island but we both agreed that we should slowly head back, drop anchor for a couple of days and assess any damage to the boat. With the steering now working we anchored as the sun rose over the reef and slept for a couple of hours. We were awakened by the sound of a boat bumping alongside. Ryan and Daniel were urgently calling me.

" 'Urricano, 'urricano come soon!!" they yelled.

"What?" I said yawning.

"Si, si, grande 'urricano en dos dias!"

Looking at the clock I saw it was just time for the Panama net, a daily radio communication on the SSB radio. I switched it on and managed to get a report that Tropical Depression Earl was off the coast of Venezuela, was probably going to be upgraded to a hurricane in a few hours and its projected path would have the eye only a hundred miles north of us – not good…

We looked at each other and immediately agreed it was time to go south as quickly as we could. I rapidly checked my repairs to the steering and Joell further secured any loose items. As Sailor again

63

looked on with dismay, I proceeded to haul up the anchor, courtesy of our powerful winch. It was now 8:45 a.m. and we needed to put as many miles between Earl and us as we could.

I gave the diesel ¾ revs and we steamed out around the island. Ten minutes later the engine exhaust changed pitch and ominous black smoke started to pour out of the engine room filling up the boat and leaving a thin layer of sticky soot everywhere....

"Shit!" I throttled back and spun the wheel. "Something's happened with the exhaust system."

Joie took the helm as we slowly headed back to the island for the second time that morning. I climbed down into the hot, sooty, exhaust-filled engine room. My flashlight peered through the gloom and exposed water and exhaust fumes gushing from the wet exhaust, where a big crack showed at the elbow. This was a new piece of heavy stainless steel I had had fabricated back at the yard in Florida and I was upset that it had appeared to fracture.

With black clouds of dirty exhaust finding their way into the salon and up on deck, we motored slowly back to a depth where we could drop the hook and I let it go in forty feet. Time was of the essence if we were to get away from the hurricane but with this problem we could go nowhere...

Joell pleaded with me not to go into the engine room as it was difficult to breathe in there but stubborn me needed to fully assess the situation immediately. Cautiously avoiding the hot engine I edged my way back to the exhaust where water was slopping up. I wrapped a rag around my hand and gingerly felt the hot metal and discovered with relief that the metal hadn't cracked, but the six-inch piece of flexible exhaust hose that joined the system together had ruptured.

64

I remembered seeing a few pieces of hose somewhere in the dark recesses of the engine room and after going on deck to gulp fresh air, I rummaged through the shelves and found a piece that I thought would work. The next half-hour was hot, grimy, uncomfortable and dirty but I removed the old hose and slid on a new piece, all the while thinking of the coming hurricane and how unstable their tracks are!

"Start the engine, Joie," I called up and as she revved slowly in neutral I could see that my repair had worked.

I jumped over the side into the warm water and scrubbed off much of the dirt and soot. With Sailor looking longingly at the island and his little doggie friend, I hauled up the anchor. It came smoothly in then suddenly stopped – it had snagged on something, probably a big piece of coral. As we were in forty feet of water there was no way I could free dive to clear it.

With Joell driving the boat slowly forward trying to dislodge the trapped anchor, the bow of the boat was being pulled down into the water. I was afraid the long bowsprit would break. Just as I was about to tell Joell to put the transmission in neutral the anchor came free and the bow of the boat shot up five feet!

"OK, that's enough excitement for one morning," I said to myself.

Luckily I had put all the necessary waypoints into the GPS a few days ago and as I always have paper charts aboard, the lack of the computerized electronic charts was no concern. After all, I had been using paper charts for over thirty years and had only bought the electronic system a few months ago.

We headed out for the third time with the wind back in the east and the waves settling down. I switched on the autopilot but all of a sudden, it wouldn't hold course at all. Ever the pragmatist, Joell said that with a hurricane barreling down on us, we'd hand steer the hundred and eighty miles! I once again crawled back to check the steering system and found that the bar connecting the sensor to the rudder had come off and was bent. In a matter of two minutes I straightened it out and re-attached it. Yay, it worked!!

All this had happened within a seven-hour period and we were pretty exhausted! I hoisted the sails and with the Perkins diesel thrumming away we headed southeast at a rapid nine knots. The first few hours were pleasant, the wind was light, the seas three feet. As night fell there was a noticeable change – the wind and waves picked up and there was lightning on the horizon.

For the next tiring twenty-four hours we had winds in the 25-30 knot range, higher in the numerous squalls that stomped over us. Seas averaged 8-10 feet with occasional groups of 12-14 footers, right on the beam. At times the rain was so intense it almost flattened the waves and the fiercely pounding raindrops made little white geysers on the surface. Although intimidating, it was breathtakingly beautiful.

We finally arrived off Isla Providencia, the haunt of pirates such as Henry Morgan. The lofty, verdant island loomed out of the squalls as a welcome sight. As we motored up the channel I doused the sails and happily hoisted the Colombian courtesy flag. We edged over to the anchorage where there was only one other sailboat. Almost immediately a launch came alongside, bearing a ship's agent, immigration, customs and sanitation inspector!

The paperwork went smoothly, with lots of smiles all around although everything on the boat, including us was soaking wet. After four years we were back in a country and amongst a people we had grown to love ...and what a captivating, charming little island this is...

TIKAL NIGHT

The night was ink-dark and motionless, but loud from the nearby roaring of a family of restless and hungry jaguars. The air was humid and the rain-forest gave off a slightly fetid aroma. The squawking of parrots and toucans, the chirping of countless insects hushed as the roars let loose again.

The four of us were perfectly still in a small clearing, standing back-to-back, facing outward. We each had a stick in our hands and we were scared, very scared. We had left the relative safety of the small hostel we were staying in near the ruins of Tikal, an ancient Mayan city in Northern Guatemala. And then we had walked a mile or so into the jungle in the middle of the night behaving like silly tourists who thought they were in Disneyland!

My friend Pete who had sailed to Guatemala with me from the Yucatan, two women we had met at the hostel, Anne and Margaret and I were going to climb one of the seven temples of Tikal to watch the sun rise above the rain forest. So we had tumbled out of bed in the early, still hours of the morning, two hours before sunrise, had gathered water bottles and walking sticks and set off single file down a narrow path toward the ruins. And then the growling started. It sounded soft at first then grew quickly.

We stopped in our tracks, petrified. Quickly, we decided to head back to the hostel but that was more than a mile away. As we hurriedly discussed our options another nerve-tingling roar came from the direction of our retreat. We couldn't go back. We shone our feeble torch beams into the jungle but they only penetrated a few feet.

So we made the decision to hold our ground and try to protect ourselves from all directions. And that is how we stood for about half-an-hour. Pressed back-to-back, occasionally shining our torch light, worried whether it might cause the predators to come closer and hoping it would scare them away. We each clutched our walking sticks tightly, not sure what we would do if a giant cat suddenly leaped out of the dark onto us.

The roaring continued for a while, seemed to get closer then further away, sometimes circling us, sometimes sounding like they were above us in the trees. After what seemed like an hour the roaring receded; they had moved off. We relaxed a little, still quite shaken, our imaginations having run riot while standing so exposed.

Ann and Margaret wanted to head straight back to the hostel, Pete and I wanted to climb the temple. It was still dark but the sun would be up in less than an hour. The women were adamant, as were we and so we split up. They headed at a run back the way we had come, Pete and I determinedly walked off in the other direction toward the temples and the still-receding roars of the beasts.

In fifteen minutes we found ourselves at the base of a mighty Mayan pyramid reaching over two hundred feet up through the rain forest. We climbed the walls, sweating in the humidity, feeling our way in the dark and occasionally turning on our nearly exhausted torches. Twenty feet from the top the walls of the temple became vertical. There was a thin, iron ladder embedded in the crumbling rock, half-rusted from many years in the humid jungle.

Pete was a big man, over 6'5" and about 240 lbs. He gave the ladder a hard pull and it resisted his shaking. So up he went, torch in mouth. Within a minute he called down that there was a small plateau there and the ladder was strong. I followed, not looking down. Out I emerged onto a ledge high above the rain forest canopy.

We sat on the smooth rock, legs dangling over the side, facing east as the sky slowly lightened, neither saying a word. The jungle below stretched as far as we could see, broken only by the tops of three other temples. Flocks of parrots flew below us, singing as the sky turned from pitch-black to the roseate hues of the dawn. Small tendrils of steam rose from the rainforest. The night sounds hushed as the sun gently spread its light over the verdant green of the jungle below.

We looked at each other and smiled. It was the most breathtaking sunrise we had ever seen or were likely to…

And the jaguars, those big cats that live in the Guatemalan jungle? We found out later, somewhat sheepishly, that the growling, howling and roaring that had so terrified us were bands of howler monkeys, so prevalent in those jungles. But even they can be dangerous, give you a nasty nip if you let them get close…

A NIGHT TO REMEMBER

After two seasons of operating my parasail business on Hilton Head Island, I sold the entire operation. I then sold my Gemini catamaran on which I had lived for two years and had cruised to Belize and Guatemala. I drove the Bugatti to Charleston, where having been vetted by Lloyds of London and proven myself capable on a trial sail to the Caribbean as first mate, I was hired as one of six delivery captains for St. Barts Yachts.

This company had won the contract with The Moorings, the largest charter yacht company in the world, to deliver new Beneteau sailboats from the nearby factory in South Carolina down to one of their many charter bases in the West Indies. The boats were trucked to Charleston, put in the water, hurriedly commissioned and then sailed non-stop about fourteen hundred miles to Tortola, St. Lucia or Grenada. As captain I was paid for each delivery but my crew were not. Generally they had some sailing knowledge, were looking for a chance to gain offshore experience and would get a free flight back to their home.

I never knew who my crew would be until three days before we were due to sail. Did they have any offshore experience (or any sailing experience at all!), would they be seasick or scared, would they do what I told them, would there be personality clashes? These questions couldn't be answered until we were at sea and there would be no turning back.

Each delivery was different – the boats ranged in size from a small 32 ft. to the luxurious 44 ft., with four cabins. We were not permitted to put up the bimini top so there was no shade or shelter in the cockpit. The plastic coverings had to be left on the cushions, we could only use one of the toilets, there was no autopilot, no radar; just get the boat there as quickly as you can and make sure it is spotless when turning it over to the base.

The weather conditions would vary from flat calm to nasty squalls and once, the edge of a hurricane. The crews included a young man in his early twenties looking for a little adventure, a homicidal Irishman, a man-hating lesbian and a multi-millionaire businessman who had always dreamed of an ocean passage. On the whole each delivery went fairly smoothly, usually the crew would mesh well and the passage would be accomplished without major problems. But there were exceptions – here is the story of one of them...

Violent Night-Miracle Morning.

My third delivery in 1994 was on a 44 ft. yacht, a comfortable and spacious design with an easy motion and a large cockpit. It was the first time I had been given command of the 'flagship' of the fleet and I was looking forward to the passage to Tortola. The first mate on this delivery had done one ocean passage before, had some sailing knowledge and could stand his watch without my checking every hour. His name was Rob and he owned a very successful electrical company in upstate New York. He was short, stocky, in his late forties, confident and pleasant.

The second mate was Bill, in his late fifties, a government employee, head of the EPA for the state of Delaware. He exuded quiet competence, had done a fair amount of coastal cruising and was looking forward to his first ocean passage out of sight of land.

We spent three days gathering provisions, going over the boat, getting to know each other, asking and answering questions. The boat was lowered into the water, the mast was stepped, the systems checked out by the shore-side crew and then early one morning in October we cast off the lines, motored down the Intracoastal Waterway a few miles and headed out to sea.

There is always a sense of exhilaration tempered with a little anxiety at the start of any offshore passage but more so in an

71

untested boat with an unknown crew. We started our watch routine, three hours on, then six hours off, although it is difficult to go below and sleep when the voyage is just beginning. I checked the boat systems again and the bilges, adjusted the run of the sheets, listened to the engine to make sure it was running smoothly, always watching my two crew members to see how they were coping.

I was fortunate with Rob and Bill – they were like eager school children and wanted to be involved with all aspects of getting the boat to its destination safely and quickly. In the first twenty four hours they proved capable of holding a steady course (we had no autopilot so the boat had to be continually hand-steered), trimming the sails, doing basic navigation and preparing edible meals. They were each interesting and well-rounded men and we three bonded very quickly into an efficient team. It seemed to me that this would be a very enjoyable, uneventful passage.

Our course was to head due east about four hundred miles out into the Atlantic where we looked for the trade winds to send us south to our destination. With a good wind, sometimes motorsailing we covered the distance in three days, found the Trades and turned south for the islands. It was late October, still in hurricane season and the forecast on the fifth day, halfway through the passage called for a squally night with winds about 25 knots and seas building a little. No hurricanes were in the vicinity.

As forecast on my portable SSB receiver the wind started to build in the afternoon and with it the seas. We sped on under reefed main and jib, hissing through the waves at six knots, watching some squalls start to develop on the horizon.

As evening approached the temperature dropped a little and the seas got bigger, the wind gusting occasionally to 30 knots, but with our foul-weather gear to keep us dry and our confidence in the boat we felt safe and secure. As dusk fell, the helmsman clipped on his safety harness and prepared for his three-hour stint at the wheel.

This night was different from the other pleasant, star-filled ones we had enjoyed. There were continual squalls now and little moonlight to spot them with. We changed the watch schedule so that there would always be one of us in the cockpit along with the helmsman to relieve him occasionally and look for squalls.

The squalls weren't particularly dangerous, usually the wind would pick up a few knots for five or ten minutes, the helmsman would bear away, some warm rain might fall. I watched Rob and Bill from the companionway and they were handling the situation well. I was very impressed with both of them and how quickly they had adapted to life at sea.

At about one in the morning, having been relieved of my watch, I stripped off my clothes and lay in my bunk trying to catch a couple of hours sleep. Wedged in with some pillows, the motion wasn't too bad and I fell asleep quickly, although with 'one eye open'. It seemed like only minutes but I awoke suddenly knowing something was desperately wrong. The boat was heeled far over and I had been slammed into the side of the cabin.

The wind was howling and the boat was groaning. There were shouts in the cockpit, they were screaming for me. I ran naked through the salon where everything had spilled out of the drawers and lockers in the knockdown. I switched on the spreader lights which illuminated the deck and clambered up the companionway steps as the boat suddenly lurched upright.

The wind noise was deafening, rain was pelting down, Bill and Rob were wild-eyed in the red glow of the compass light and bedlam reigned. My eyes were instantly drawn to the compass so I could get an idea of our heading. I saw something I had never

73

seen in twenty years of sailing and hoped to never see again – the compass was slowly going around and around...But it wasn't the compass – that stays fixed on magnetic north – it was the boat!

The reefed mainsail was slamming the boom from one side to another as the boat spun slowly in circles. Bill was struggling with the wheel and kept getting knocked to his knees. Rob was trying to furl in the small area of jib that had been up but was having little success. I stood there for two seconds taking all this in, immediately buckled my safety harness over my bare chest and leaped into the cockpit.

The wind must have been blowing over seventy knots, almost hurricane force and looking out, all I could see was a wall of spume and rain around us. The wind in the rigging was making an awful noise, so loud that I had to shout from two feet away to be heard.

"Sails down – NOW!" I yelled.

I grabbed the furling line and wrapped it around the nearest winch. Rob ground it in, with me tailing, sheets cracking and after thirty seconds the jib was furled. Bill wrestled with the wheel but the reefed main was making the boat unmanageable. I reached down and turned on the engine, quickly looked to make sure no ropes or lines were trailing in the water and jammed it into gear.

"Try to keep a straight course," I shouted into Bill's ear.

"I'll try, but the wind's going in circles!"

"Got to get the main down," I yelled loudly again.

And then on that wildly bucking boat, in a maelstrom of wind and waves, the warm rain beating on me, with the boat turning circles, I clipped my safety harness onto the mast and climbed out of the cockpit. Without the protection of the dodger I was fully exposed to the wind, which tried to blow me off the boat.

I clawed my way to the mast in the dark.

"Release the main halyard-RELEASE IT NOW!" I yelled.

I pulled on the luff of the main and inch by inch it came down. On my knees on top of the coachroof I somehow managed to tie some gaskets around the mainsail securing it to the boom. I crawled back and fell into the cockpit, totally exhausted, totally drenched, still totally naked…

And then it all stopped; the wind, the rain, the noise, the spinning. I looked up and saw a star-filled inky-black sky. I looked behind and saw a towering wall of wind and water and rain receding. The seas continued their wild anger. Bill's eyes were huge and Rob vomited.

"What the hell was that?" Bill asked.

"I don't know, I've never seen anything like it," I replied.

Rob did not look well so I ordered him to his cabin. He didn't want to go, said it was still his watch, but I insisted. The wind was now only blowing about twenty knots, Bill and I got the cockpit sorted out, cleaned up the mess, hoisted the reefed main, unfurled a bit of jib and set course for Tortola still about seven days sail away.

Bill's teeth were chattering, in fact his whole body was shaking, so I told him to get a couple of hours sleep, I'd get dressed and take over his watch. He went below and I steered through the night trying to fathom what had happened to us. About four in the morning, Bill relieved me, said Rob still wasn't feeling well, but he would steer by himself for a while. I went below, curled up in my mess of a cabin and tried to get an hour of sleep. It seemed that no sooner had I closed my eyes than Bill was shaking me awake.

"Jon, we've got a very sick man on board, Rob is in agony."

I hove the boat to, so she would not sail anywhere but remain in a comfortable position relative to the waves. Rob was laying in his cabin in the fetal position breathing heavily. My eyes were drawn to his hands – his fingers were like claws, frozen into a grotesque position. He was very pale, sweaty, but conscious.

"Get some wet towels," I told Bill. He went to the galley to find some.

"What's wrong, Rob, do you know what's hurting you?"

"Kidney stone," he gasped.

"How do you know?"

"I was in the hospital two weeks ago; they said it would pass on its own."

"Has it passed?" I asked him.

"No, it's still there."

"Do you have pain medication?"

"No, I didn't bring it with."

Here we were, hundreds of miles from land with a man in extreme agony and all I had on board were some aspirin! Rob put on a brave front, said he'd be alright soon and wanted to stand his watch!

We put the cool towels on his forehead and I told Bill to keep an eye on him. I looked over my charts but I already knew that St. Thomas was the closest port and that was six days away. With only a VHF radio, I could transmit no further than about twenty miles, so I was truly on my own. I didn't know if his condition would worsen, I didn't know if Rob would die out there.

I went back on deck and set a course for the islands, shaking out a further reef in the main. I told Bill to rest and that I would wake him in two hours. He had wedged Rob into his bunk with some cushions, given him some water and there was no more we could do for him. As dawn lightened the sky I could see the clouds were low and scudding and visibility was down to a couple of miles. It was a grey, bleak seascape, with six foot waves and blowing spume. I sat at the wheel, exhausted and scared for Rob, with no way of contacting anyone.

Bill came and relieved me, his eyes bloodshot, still shaky from the nightmare a few hours before. I went below and plotted our position on the chart and was about to grab an apple when Bill yelled at me.

"Come on deck, Captain - right away!"

"Oh no, what's happened now?" I thought.

I clambered up the steps and as my head reached the cockpit, Bill had a big grin on his face and was pointing behind us. I couldn't believe what I was seeing! Here we were, hundreds of miles out in the Atlantic, nowhere near the regular shipping lanes and two miles behind us, coming out of a squall was a big white cruise ship! I thought it was a mirage, the residual effect of an incredibly stressful few hours, lack of sleep, too much worry.

But no, it was real and was proceeding at about 20 knots across our stern. I jumped below and switched on the VHF radio.

"Cruise ship, cruise ship, this is the yacht Beneteau, do you read me?"

"Beneteau, this is the Royal Caribbean, we read you and have a visual."

"Royal Caribbean, I have a medical emergency aboard and request to speak with the ship doctor."

"Stand by."

I waited by the radio, then Bill called down to me "Jon, she's changing course towards us!"

"Beneteau, Beneteau, this is Royal Caribbean, do you read me?"

"Loud and clear."

"Beneteau, I have the ship's doctor standing by."

A rich Scottish accent came over the radio,

"Kiptin, how kin ah hilp you?"

"Doctor, I have a white male, 53 years old in severe pain with a kidney stone. His hands are claw-shaped, he hasn't moved from the fetal position for hours and he's sweating profusely."

He asked me how I knew it was a kidney stone and what medicines we had on board. I told him only aspirin and I was concerned that Rob's condition was life-threatening.

"Noo", said the doctor, "it's nah life-threatenin', but it is extremely painful, which is whah his hands are rigid."

We talked some more and then he asked me to stand by. I went up to the cockpit for a moment and couldn't believe what I saw. Standing off from us about five hundred yards, having altered course and slowed down, was this huge cruise ship placidly ignoring the waves which were still bouncing us around.

The decks were lined with people, even at this early hour. I imagined word must have spread around the ship and passengers wanted to take pictures and look at this tiny yacht tossing about on the stormy seas.

The radio crackled to life and the doctor came back on.

"Kiptin, the only thing you kin do to hilp this man on yeer boat is to keep cooling him down and give him aspirin. He may or may not pass the kidney stoon, but he *will* be OK. Did anything happen that might have caused the stoon to move, did he fall doon recently?"

I briefly described the pounding we had taken a few hours earlier and he agreed that had probably caused the stone to loosen.

"Kiptin, please stand by, there is someone here who wants to talk to you an' goood luck to you."

There was a moment's pause and then a distinguished British voice with a clipped accent came over the speaker.

"Captain White, this is Captain Jamison of the Royal Caribbean."

I immediately smoothed my hair down and sat straighter on the bench!

"Yes, Captain, thank you for altering course and rendering assistance."

"It appears that you have the situation under control, but if you wish, we could lower a boat and bring your crew member aboard. My only concern is that the seas are running about six feet and it may be more perilous to transfer him."

I looked out at the ocean and thought about moving Rob from his cabin up the companionway steps, across the cockpit and then getting him safely lowered into a boat tied alongside bouncing around in the waves. The doctor had said that Rob's condition was not life-threatening.

"Captain, I thank you for your offer but I agree that it would be more risky to transfer him than to take care of him here. The doctor says he'll eventually be alright and my other crew and I can take care of him."

"Captain White, you seem to have everything under control, what will you do if the man's condition deteriorates?"

"I have thought of that and if necessary, I will activate my Emergency Position Radio Beacon. We should be in range of a Coast Guard helicopter from Puerto Rico."

"Yes, that was my thought as well. I wish you a safe passage, Captain White and good luck."

"Thank you Captain and again, many thanks to you and the Doctor for your assistance – you were a Godsend..."

With hundreds of people waving and a blast of her horns the ship churned up the seas with her propellers and within minutes was out of sight. The weather soon started to clear and by midday we were back to blue skies, puffy white clouds and a steady trade wind breeze.

We cleaned up the jumble that the knockdown had produced and looked in on Rob every few minutes. He seemed to be doing better, the pain was subsiding, his hands were unclenching. In fact, he desperately wanted to resume his watch but I told him the doctor insisted he rest for a day.

We finished the delivery a few days later, Rob feeling weak but enthusiastic about the adventure and with stories to tell his grandchildren. The three of us enjoyed a beer at The Moorings base in Tortola and discussed the events of that night. We all agreed we had been hit head on by a huge, dangerous waterspout, the ocean equivalent of a tornado…

SAD SALLY

I lived on a small barrier island off the coast of South Carolina for a while. It is known as Daufuskie Island and was the actual location of Pat Conroy's bestseller "The Water Is Wide". He called it Yamacraw Island in the book and movie.

The island has changed little in the thirty years since he taught the natives there. A parcel of the land has been turned into an exclusive resort with a golf course and a smattering of large estate homes. The development has been losing huge sums of money since its inception.

Most of the island is undeveloped, unpaved and unkempt. The roads are sandy trails which become quagmires when it rains. There are old black families living in ramshackle houses and cabins and mobile homes, families whose ancestors were slaves and grew the famed Sea Island cotton. They drink and make babies and fight among themselves and sometimes shoot each other.

There are a few dozen white folk living in the unspoiled, almost inaccessible parts of the island. Some of them take the ferry to nearby Hilton Head Island to work in the tourist industry. Some of them take the tourists from Hilton Head on bus tours around Daufuskie – the visitors usually look bored and hot and sweaty from a bumpy two hours in a steamy, rattling twenty-year old yellow school bus. They are glad to get back on the air-conditioned ferry, having seen but not understood what they saw.

I lived with Sally, a tall, willowy blonde artist who was much in demand for her exquisite portraits. She came from an old-monied South Carolina family and her ancestors probably owned the ancestors of the black families who lived down the road. Her house was ancient and crooked and parts of it showed her creative touch. It was a mile down a rutted lane, impassible in the winter when the heavy rains continually washed out the road.

We would park her battered truck and pick our way to the house at night with feeble flashlights barely lighting the way through trees hanging with Spanish moss and scrub tearing at our ankles. The house stood alone in a small clearing among the pines, on a spit of land called Rams Horn Bluff. It was beautiful, peaceful and serene. It was also full of mosquitoes and snakes.

Our relationship was intense and sporadic for we only spent about ten days a month together. At the time I was a professional captain delivering sailboats to the Caribbean. I would be off on a voyage for a couple of weeks, then come back to Sally for a few days and be gone again. Sally had an eleven-year old son who was a 'difficult' child. He had no father and did not relate well to the few other kids on the island. He wasted most of his time playing violent video games.

He liked me and I liked him. I spent time with him, gave him my telescope, tried to cure him of his lazy ways. Most of the time it didn't work. I like to think that for the few months I was in his life I contributed something positive – some of the islanders told me later that I had.

Sally was the saddest woman I ever knew. She was content with her sadness, it cloaked her with an aura, a mystery which she perpetuated as much as she could. She had a vision of herself as she perceived others saw her. She described it to me a couple of months into our relationship.

"I'm the strange, sad artist who lives in the woods with her weird son."

I tried to make her laugh and occasionally I succeeded. But as time passed I realized that she liked this image of herself and cultivated it to the point where she became her perception and all the world saw her as strange, sad Sally.

When it became apparent that nothing I could say or do would make her happy I knew it was time to end this relationship. I told her I could give her no more of my laughter and that we must move in different directions. She lashed out at her son, yelling that it was all his fault, that he had driven me away.

Sad Sally blamed him for everything that had gone wrong in her life and because of that she hated him and he hated her. I believe they still live on Rams Horn Bluff, she's still painting and he probably plays ever-more violent video games. And the road is still washed out in winter…

A CATAMARAN LOST AT SEA

Cartagena in August – very hot, very humid, very lovely. After having JoJo, our 32' Fisher catamaran hauled at a small boatyard and getting her painted a bright blue/green, we were back at the little Club Nautico Marina. We had been in Cartagena for a couple of months enjoying this popular Colombian tourist city with its ancient fortifications, meandering alleys, street performers and living history. A vibrant, thrumming place we felt safe and welcome but it was time to move somewhere else and we weren't sure where.

A large catamaran expertly backed into a vacant space just behind us and after helping them tie up and get the 'lay of the land', the Captain, John (Whitey) White invited us aboard. He and his wife Max operated the 52ft. catamaran in the charter fleet and were heading back from a season in Panama to the Virgin Islands. We quickly became friends and over a barbeque on their large aft deck, Whitey announced that the noble little JoJo would make an excellent one-couple charter boat and we should head to Tortola and participate in the annual yacht charter show, where booking agents come from all over the world to check out what's available for the upcoming season.

He made a phone call and found out there was one spot available which he promptly booked for us. Whitey and Max were legends in the charter business and if he recommended us then that was good enough for the organizers. The show was only eight weeks away and it was a thousand miles of hard sailing against the wind the whole way. But after a brief discussion, Joell and I decided to go for it and become a charter business! We sent in a small deposit to hold our location and made preparations for the arduous passage ahead.

The voyage north along the coast of Colombia is dangerous for a number of reasons. There are few places to stop and refuel, the coast is full of pirates in swift pangas, the wind and current would be against us and the flotsam from the giant River Magdalena is swept many miles out to sea and is a huge hazard. We were warned by sailors who had knew these waters that this passage was considered the most difficult in the Caribbean and bigger yachts than ours had been defeated by the adverse conditions.

We helped Whitey, Max and their crew of three young 'hitchhikers' cast off from the rickety docks and told them we'd be a few days behind them and would see them in Tortola. Two days later as we were loading provisions for the voyage, news came through that a large catamaran had sunk off the Colombian coast.

There was a lot of misinformation and rumour but a few hours later we learned that Whitey's boat had hit what they assumed was a container that had fallen off a cargo ship and they had abandoned the lovely boat as it filled with water. They took to the life raft and after a harrowing experience were rescued by a freighter then air lifted by helicopter to the Virgin Islands. We were in shock, as was the entire sailing community but luckily no one was seriously hurt.

We motored over to the fuel dock, topped off our tank and five-gallon containers and sailed back past the marina and out of Cartagena Bay into the Caribbean.

Right away we knew we were in for a rough trip as the wind blew from the north and kicked up a short, steep chop with a serried repetitiveness we would come to hate over the next week. We had secured everything inside the boat but we bounced around as JoJo rocked like a bucking bronco, the nasty three foot waves slamming into the bridgedeck with a force and continuity that I thought would break and defeat her. Night came and we motored into the wind about five miles off the coast. Our course was northeast and that's the direction the wind blew from – right on the nose.

The next day found us about seventy miles up the coast with some strange sights in front of us. I called Joell and we both looked through binoculars at vast islands ahead where the chart showed open ocean. As I slowed the throttle we came upon a small island that floated by on our port side. It was made up of grass and tree limbs and plants and branches, a little floating land mass. The next one was much larger and as we scanned the horizon, there were hundreds of islands in front of us, as far as we could see.

Checking the chart I found we were about ten miles south of the delta for the Rio Magdalena, the huge river that starts in the foothills of the Andes and travels nearly 1000 miles north collecting natural and man-made debris in its path. This was the barrier now in front of us. We had been told that the debris can stretch twenty miles from the delta and we had found it.

With Joell up in the bow, holding on tight as the wind and waves battered the bows we weaved our way through the immense and bizarre landscape (seascape?!). She would call out "Hard to port" and I would spin the wheel.

Then "Go straight, no – a little starboard".

Sometimes a trailing branch would scrape along the side and I would wince, thinking about our new paint. I was concerned about long vines or pieces of rope catching in the propeller. It was hot, exhausting, slow work, but after several hours we were through the maze and the seas ahead were clear. I pushed the throttle up and we proceeded north east against the wind and current, bouncing and pitching at about 3 knots made good.

We were going through fuel faster than I had anticipated and although we didn't want to we knew we would have to stop somewhere and top up the tanks. But where on this coast was safe? Just past the delta of the Rio Magdelana and the town of Barranquilla, the coast makes a sharp turn inland and forms a large bight about 50 miles across.

As it was getting dark we decided to continue directly to Santa Marta, seventy miles along the coast. We felt that there was less chance of being spotted by pirates further offshore, at night with our running lights off.

And so we powered through the starry night, the wind slacked a little, the waves were not quite so vicious. Joell occupied her time wedged into a corner, stitching pillows. I drowsed at the wheel, watched for other boats and occasionally filled the diesel tank from our five gallon jerry cans.

As dawn cleared the darkness, land lay directly ahead. I had set a course for a little bay thinking it would offer protection from the northeast trade winds so we could rest. I inched our way into deserted Bahia 'Inca- Inca' and dropped the anchor. We both fell instantly asleep.

We were awakened a few hours later by tapping on the hull – it was a group of kids in a leaky panga. They wanted to come aboard and we invited them, watching that they didn't steal anything. They turned out to be great boys and all they wanted was pencils and paper for school. I told them I needed to fill our jerry cans with diesel and they offered to take me ashore to a gas station.

After making sure the boat was anchored well and Joell was OK, I headed to shore with them, two of the kids constantly bailing the leaky boat. There was a little village with one gas station and we traipsed up there, filled the cans and staggered back to their panga. A short row and we were back aboard JoJo where Joell had been entertaining two of the yongsters.

We loaded them up with school supplies and candy, lots of hugs and handshakes, they watched while we got the anchor up and then rowed as hard as they could for a mile waving and cheering.

Rounding the headland the wind and waves picked up and we again settled into the monotonous routine of up and down, up and down, slamming of water, jostling of everything aboard. The dinghy which was tied on the foredeck broke loose and I made my way cautiously up forward to capture and re-secure it before it damaged the boat or itself.

Five miles offshore with Santa Marta to starboard, doggedly paralleling the coast, brave little JoJo bucked on. The Yanmar diesel purred at 2000 rpm, the prop spun and spun, occasionally rising to a high pitch as a particularly steep wave caused it to cavitate out of the water.

Past Riohacho in the darkness, the dawn showing more dry landscape off to starboard. I constantly scanned the coastline and out to sea for signs of lone craft, our pirate experience in Costa Rica the year before still fresh in my mind. Two more days and nights and we passed Bahia Hondita at the northernmost point in Colombia and South America. Now we looked at an eerie, desert landscape with no trees and no sign of human habitation. We turned more to the east…and so did the wind!

Aruba was 150 miles away, right into the wind. It took two more days and nights of pounding and slamming, fifty hours where we got thrown around, bruised and psychologically beaten up but finally one bright and sunny morning we slowly motored into Oranjestad harbor and tied up at customs.

JoJo had done it, had battled some of the most uncomfortable conditions we had experienced for six nights and seven days but we were there, with only another 600 miles against the wind, into the northeast trades to get to Tortola…and that's another story!

HARLEM IN PAKISTAN

Stumbling out of the dim, smoky, spice-laden milieu of the bazaar, I found myself back on the main thoroughfare in Peshawar, western Pakistan. The sky outside was brilliant blue, the air was hot and clammy and just ahead of me a large group of people were surrounding a vehicle, jabbering loudly and gesticulating.

With my hippy look of faded jeans, tatty T-shirt and sandals, long hair and Jerry Garcia beard, the crowd was momentarily diverted as they pointed at me, then turned their attention back to the car. I pushed my way through them and was astounded at what I saw. Inside a fairly old VW Squareback sporting German license plates, were four black guys, eyes wide and white with fear.

The driver rolled down his window and asked if I spoke English. On hearing my British accent he and his friends looked relieved, opened the two doors and piled out into the street. To the stupefied gaze of the crowd of Pakistanis and me, they proceeded to uncoil until we were all looking up at four big dudes from Harlem, the shortest of whom was 6'6" – this in a country where 5'9" is considered very tall! They all had frizzy Afros and gold chains and their fear was replaced with smiles. I proceeded to do the customary handshake, palm grip etc. with all of them and then they looked around, as the crowd grew quiet.

"Look man," the tallest said to me, "we're almost out of gas and we don't have any money – we're heading to India and you can ride all the way to Delhi if you can put some gas in the car".

I didn't have much money, but gas was cheap and this seemed too surreal to pass up.

"OK," I replied. "As long as I can drive, you're on."

They immediately started slapping me on the back, then one of them reached into the car and brought out a tube of rolled fabric.

He proceeded to lay out four prayer rugs and these very tall guys bent down and facing Mecca, began praying to Allah. Having recently been assured by an Afghan tribesman that Moslems were peace-loving and accepting people, I took this in stride. The crowd of Pakistanis however, did not.

They now knew these guys were Americans and apparently assumed that they were making fun of Islam. One Pakistani started yelling and shaking his fist, as the men continued in their prayers. Then they all started shouting and pointing. I got a little nervous and when a Pakistani landed a blow on one of the big guys, they finally got the message too. Like lightning, they jumped up, threw their prayer rugs into the station wagon and scrambled inside, as I flung myself into the driver seat, started her up, put her in gear and floored it.

Angry, startled Pakistanis leaped out of the way as I barreled down the street, swerving to miss rickety old buses, wandering cows and creaking rickshaws. I looked to my right and then glanced into the back seat, where there was a bundle of intermingled arms, legs and wide grins.

"Man, we got outathere just in time," one of them said.

"Looks like you can drive real good."

"Yeah, I can," said I. "I've got a feeling we're going to have a few adventures before we get to Delhi."

And we did ...

'IMAGINE' AND THE KU KLUX KLAN

In the autumn of 1992 I single-handed my 41' Searunner trimaran 'Imagine' from Jacksonville, Florida up the Intracoastal Waterway to Hilton Head Island, S.C. My girlfriend Lyndy and I had parted ways and I was heading back to the dock I had cast off from almost three years earlier. I had had many adventures sailing through the Caribbean and down to Venezuela but it was time to settle down for a while and replenish the cruising kitty.

The weather was perfect, a slight NW breeze with sultry fall temperatures, as my trusty engine pushed me at a comfortable five knots across a large estuary near Sapelo Sound in Georgia. An occasional powerboat passed me heading south, the harbinger of the hundreds of snowbirds who would soon be crowding the waterway, escaping from the northern winter to the warmth of Florida and the Bahamas. The shrimping fleet was combing the waters of this broad and peaceful bay, slowly moving in rhythmical patterns against the south-moving current.

I felt relaxed and happy, only another two days to go and I would be back with old friends at a familiar little marina. A loud bang, a shudder, the engine abruptly stopped! I threw the transmission into neutral and pushed the engine start button. The Yanmar diesel fired right up, but when I put her in gear, she promptly quit - a line might have wrapped round the propeller.

The boat slowed and then started moving backward with the current. I ran to the foredeck and heaved the anchor over the side. It caught immediately in the soft muck of the bottom. Looking over the stern, there was a crab trap bobbing about five feet behind, its rope wrapped around my propeller. One of the hazards of the waterway had snared me!

The current was running strong now, over two knots and I was concerned about being swept away when I went into the water to cut the line free. A shrimp boat hailed me on the radio.

"You OK, Cap'n?" he enquired in a voice like Bubba Gump.

 I told him my situation and that I had to go over the side and cut
the trap free. He said he would stand by in case I got into trouble.
A few minutes later, as I was tying a line around my waist, his big
old shrimp boat pulled up nearby and the Captain waved at me.

We spoke on the radio a little, then knife in hand, I jumped off
the back of the boat into the warm, brown, swiftly moving water.
I had to quickly pull myself back to the boat as it was near the
height of the ebb tide and the current was fast.

I managed to get under the boat and felt the rope wrapped tightly
around the prop shaft. I hacked at it several times, holding my
breath as long as I could, fighting the current pushing at me.
Finally, I was able to unravel it all and the crab pot took off in the
current, heading for its own adventures!

My concern was if the rope had done any damage to the shaft or
strut, so I gingerly felt along them and oh no! – the strut which
kept the shaft straight had snapped in two. I was immobile; there
was no way to use the motor…

I climbed back on deck, tired and concerned. I was in the middle
of nowhere, miles from any facility and it would be dark soon. I
let the shrimper know my situation and told him I would remain
there at anchor overnight until I figured out what to do. He told
me he'd check back in the morning, blew his horn and steamed
slowly off.

Another voice came over the VHF radio, a slow, southern drawl
telling me he had been listening to my radio talk with the
shrimper.

"Cap'n," he said slowly, "Mah name's Bear an' ah live on a small islan' 'bout four miles south of where I reckon you is. Now, if'n you can sail that boat of yours back here, well, I got a dock an' mebbe we can fix yer trouble."

He told me it was called Palm Island and I found it on my chart. It was only a few miles back off the main waterway but to get there meant I had to sail a boat 41' long and 24' wide through some small, meandering unmarked channels.

With about three hours of daylight left, I told him I would attempt to make it to his place and he said he had a small boat to tow me the last few hundred feet if I needed it. The current would help me and the wind would be behind. I cleared everything off the decks, got the jib ready to unfurl the instant the anchor was weighed and went forward to pull the anchor up.

In those days I was pretty fit and there was no anchor windlass on the boat. But with a two-knot current pushing the boat against the anchor, there was no way I could manhandle the anchor aboard. And without the engine to power against the current, I wasn't going anywhere...

It took me fifteen minutes to rig up a block-and-tackle, leading the heavy anchor rope to a main winch. There followed a painful hour, slowly grinding the winch, hauling up the anchor inch-by-inch. The current was slacking off, the mosquitoes were coming out and with a Herculean effort, I pulled the muddy chain and anchor aboard, ran back to the cockpit, unfurled the genoa and turned the boat south, wiping rivers of sweat off me.

With the wind behind and the current with me, I sailed back down the ICW at five knots. It was very tranquil, gliding silently past the tall rushes and occasional oak tree. I located the small channel off the waterway, which would lead me to Palm Island and calculated that I could use the wind to negotiate the winding passage most of the way.

As I sailed slowly down the first channel I called 'Bear' on the radio to see if he knew the depths. He told me that shrimp boats sometimes came through that channel, so it should be deep enough for me.

Cranking up the centerboard, the boat now drew less than three feet. I was confident that I had enough water underneath me but as I rounded a bend into another channel and adjusted the sails, I looked ahead and my heart stopped. There was a lone telephone wire strung overhead…

"Bear, Bear!" I called frantically into the radio, "what's the clearance on that telephone line ahead of me?"

"Well now, I don' rightly know that, Cap. But lak ah said, the shrimp boats sumptimes go down there…"

"Great, they don't have a mast sticking fifty-three feet into the air!" I thought.

By this time, I was close to it and it looked too low to clear. The tide was falling, I was committed and held my breath. In the middle of nowhere, with tall reeds limiting my horizon, with no one around, at dusk on a beautiful Georgia evening the gods smiled on Imagine and me as we glided under that obstacle with the VHF antenna making brief contact and snapping back!

Major sigh of relief and I steered the boat into ever smaller and narrower channels, following the chart and Bear's directions on the radio. He could now see my mast and would come to guide me in.

A few minutes later a little skiff with an outboard came into view and this big, bearded, southern cracker with a large grin and a couple of missing teeth tossed me a line and slowly towed me to the ramshackle dock on the island.

We tied Imagine up and shook hands. Here I was stranded on an island in the middle of the South with a character out of Deliverance!

We went up to the house and I met his wife Betty, who made a fuss of me and got me an ice-cold beer. She was pretty, but tired-looking, with sun-bleached blonde hair and happy wrinkles lining her face.

The house was large and rambling and the grounds well kept, a long lawn leading down to the water with many oak trees draped with Spanish moss. I was curious as to how they could afford such a magnificent place and they told me they were the caretakers for a rich family from Savannah, who came to the island occasionally to get away.

They were delighted to have company and told me I could have my own room and could stay as long as I liked. Not to worry, Bear's brother had a portable welding machine and he'd call him tomorrow, see what could be done to fix my boat...

We went for a long walk as the sun set and the bugs came out. This place was a little paradise, with peacocks roaming, a herd of tame, friendly deer, beautiful meadows and meandering creeks. It was quiet, primitive and spectacular, on oasis of peace far from noise, pollution and stress.

Over a sumptuous southern dinner they listened spellbound to my stories of sailing the Caribbean, of trekking the snow-topped mountains in Venezuela, and of the wild New Year's Eve at Foxy's on Jost Van Dyke. Their world was limited by the boundary of Georgia, a state they had never been out of. As the night wore on, we sat on the screened-in porch, drinking beer and feeling comfortable.

"So, Bear, where are we going to haul 'Imagine' out?"

There was no boatyard around so how were we to expose the bottom of the boat to fix it?

"No problem," said Bear, "there's a sand spit a hundred yards down, we'll tow yer boat there at high tide, anchor her down and when the tide goes out, she'll be high 'n dry."

Life couldn't be much better, I thought, these people were gracious in their own rough way, the island was a sanctuary, and my boat would get repaired.

Over one last beer, we started to talk about life in the south and Bear casually mentioned that he was a card-carrying member of the KKK! I tried not to bat an eye, but my mind instantly went back to a similar situation in Afghanistan over twenty years earlier, when I had been confronted by a tall, fiercely-armed Afghani tribesman who had demanded to know my religion...

Betty could see I was a little bit uncomfortable, so she ushered me off to my room where I instantly fell asleep to the droning of the mosquitoes and bugs outside my window, the frogs bellowing sadly into the night. The next morning, after a huge breakfast, Bear called his brother who said he'd be pleased to come to the island to fix the problem for the sailing Cap'n.

I accompanied Bear on his morning chores, hand-feeding the deer, clearing some brush, drinking some beer. In the afternoon, he took a couple of rifles and taught me how to shoot. He was amazed that I had never shot a gun before, couldn't understand why folks in England didn't all have firearms.

"What was it, a Commie country?"

He asked me if they had a Klan coven in England and I told him I didn't think so. We're out in the woods, me and this big old redneck with rifles and live ammunition, talking about the KKK – it was a little surreal, to say the least.

And then he started talking about his church and Jesus! He asked me what church I belonged to – how do I get myself into these situations!? I looked him square in the eye and told him I was a Jew. I figured I had about ten seconds to live, but after a moment's shock, he grinned really big, slapped his arm around my shoulder and told me to stop joking with him.

"No, Bear", I said, holding my ground, "I am."

"Naw, you cain't be, yur a good guy and yur from Engiland."

"Well Bear, seems to me that there's good and bad people everywhere, good and bad Jews and Christians and Moslems. Good and bad blacks and whites, yellow and brown. Good and bad Englishmen and rednecks from Georgia! And Bear, you're a good redneck from Georgia, even if we're miles apart on how we look at life."

He thought for a minute, picked up his rifle, shot at a tree a hundred yards away and turned back to look at me, squinting his eyes.

"Well, Cap'n, I reckon you're right 'bout that, but I never thought ah'd ever meet a Jew in mah life, 'specially here on this little biddy islan'. An' I lak you, so let's walk on back to the house and have a couple of beers, quench our thirst…"

And that's what we did, this big hulking redneck, tattoos, missing teeth, greasy beard, rifle slung over his shoulder and the long-haired, bearded, English, Jewish sailing Captain…

We talked for hours, he wanted to know so much about the world beyond the marshes and the waterways and I told him of the countries I'd traveled through, some of the people I'd met in India and Australia and South America. We were very relaxed with each other and Betty fussed over us with beer and food, delighted that Bear was being educated about a world he never knew existed.

The next day we went to get his brother Bill, cruising the skiff through narrow, unmarked channels for an hour, until we came to a small, run-down dock in a small, run-down town. There he was, with welding gear, a big tank, rods, all the necessary items to repair my broken strut. He was an easy-going man, more educated than Bear, pleased to help out a man in distress.

And it happened as we had discussed; we towed Imagine out to the sandbar, let the tide drop away exposing the damage and crouched in the moist sand.

Bill went to work and in an hour had straightened and welded the strut. Waiting for the tide to float her off, we sat and drank beer and watched spellbound as a lone dolphin swam by and looked directly at us…a good omen, I thought.

When Imagine was afloat, I started the engine and gingerly put her in gear. If the strut had not been welded exactly straight, there would be a vibration which could knock the engine and transmission off their mounts. Slowly the boat moved forward under her own power.

There was no vibration, the shaft was running true and I hadn't done damage to the gears. We had a great dinner that evening, I was high as a kite. Everyone was happy and Bill would not accept a penny for his work – he was just pleased to be able to help me and asked that I do the same for someone else. I liked that man; in fact I liked them all!

The next morning, slightly hung over, I waited for the tide to drop a little to be sure I would clear the telephone line.

With hugs and promises to stay in touch, I pulled away from the dock, turned Imagine around in the narrow channel, waved farewell and headed back to the ICW to end my journey in Hilton Head.

The next day, only twenty miles from home, in a narrow part of the ICW, I nodded to a man fishing in a small skiff. As I turned back, there was an ominous bang, a loud screeching sound and the Yanmar diesel abruptly stopped. Out went the anchor again and I scrambled below into the tiny engine room. This time, it was fatal – the engine had apparently thrown a rod! After three years and thousands of miles, so close to home, she died on me.

I got on the radio and managed to get through to a friend on Hilton Head, who said he'd come and tow me back. The fisherman in the skiff came over to chat and I invited him aboard for a beer.

He was a quiet, rather sullen man, who told me over the second beer that he'd been released from prison a couple of months earlier.

"What were you in jail for?" I asked.

"Murder," he replied…

THE LAST GREAT ROCK FESTIVAL

The summer of 1970 was the last 'summer of love'. The huge influx of American hippies traveling Europe would diminish after that summer and the era of 'peace and love' would be shattered by the evil of Charles Manson, the killing of four students at Kent State and the winding down of the Vietnam War.

I was in my second year at Temple University in Philadelphia, studying how to throw great parties, skip class and stay out of the army! There was a charter flight arranged by the University to go to London in June and I, along with some friends, bought a ticket and looked forward to a "groovy" time. On the flight over the captain informed us that we would likely be searched by customs at Gatwick Airport. Instantly joints were lit up and people started popping pills, so they wouldn't be busted in England! I don't think that's what the captain had in mind...

I bought a used Triumph 650 motorcycle and spent a few weeks touring the English countryside. Then I decided to sell it and hitchhike around Europe. Three weeks before I was due to fly home, I found myself back in England and headed to the Isle of Wight, a large island just off the south coast of England.

Word had spread all over Europe that there was to be a giant rock festival to rival Woodstock, to be held on the island before the summer ended and hundreds of thousands of hippies were expected to attend. Having been at Woodstock the previous year and not remembering too much of it, I looked forward to actually seeing and hearing the dozens of rock groups who were to perform.

When I arrived at the site, after taking a ferry and bus, I found that work had just begun and the festival was due to start in only nineteen days! I pitched my tent in the middle of what was to become a totally packed field and wandered over to where some construction was starting.

I sat on the grass with a couple of other guys and we discussed whether we could make some money working on the site. The next day we were hired to help erect the corrugated iron fence that was supposed to keep the non-paying attendees out. We dug trenches in the ground and helped maneuver the fencing into place. The second day at lunch time, I was sitting by myself near the entrance to the festival.

A beautiful, black Jaguar 420 pulled up next to me and a large man with long blond hair got out. He walked over and asked me if I was working for the festival. I told him I was and he wanted to know if I could help him with a problem.

"Sure," I said. "What do you need?"

"I'm Ricky Farr and I'm the producer of the festival. This fence looks bloody awful. I want you to go into town and buy as much paint and as many brushes as you can get. Can you do that?"

"Absolutely I can. Where do I go and how do I get there?"

"Go into Freshwater and Shanklin and wherever you need to and get back here quick. Here's the key to the Jag. Can you drive a stick?"

"No worries, Mr. Farr, but how do I pay for this?"

"I have accounts at the major ironmongers – here are the addresses and here's a note from me. They can call me at the office on-site to confirm, OK?"

I drove to the nearby town of Freshwater and loaded gallons of paint into the boot. Then I drove to Shanklin and putting a tarp on the back seat, squeezed every inch with more paint cans, brushes and rollers.

I drove back to the site at Afton Down and found Ricky in his office. He was busy, but told me to find his 'sidekick' Jeff Dexter who would tell me what to do. I found him, an elf-like, busy young man and he gave me a big wad of festival tickets. He told me to find people who would paint different things on the fence, preferably flowers and peace signs and psychedelic motifs that hippies like. I would pay them by giving them free tickets.

"Can you do that, mate?" he asked.

"'Course I can," I replied, happily.

I set up an area next to the main entrance, got myself an official pass and handed out paint cans and a brush to whoever wanted them. The next few days were immense fun and I became very popular as the campgrounds began to rapidly fill up and word spread that there was a bloke handing out free tickets! As tickets for the five-day festival cost the equivalent of $30, there was no shortage of willing help! I probably handed out over five hundred tickets...

I instructed everyone to paint something positive and attractive to cover the bleak expanse of grey fence. Some areas were works of art, with intricate patterns and designs. Some were raunchy with 'FUCK THE PIGS' in large letters. On the whole it came out alright and I was thrilled to be giving out all those free tickets, plus I had a pass to every part of backstage for the whole event!

On Wednesday, the day before the show, I went into the office to let Ricky know we were out of paint and the job was as good as it would get.

"Good job, mate. Tell you what – think you could help out a bit when the performers arrive? Make sure they get to the tents and their caravans. See if they need anything special, look after them a bit."

"Yes, Ricky, I think I could do that…"

And I did.

I made sure Joni Mitchell had some wine, Jim Morrison some beer. Jimi Hendrix had all the dope he needed, there was nothing I could help him with! The Moody Blues stayed in their dark blue van, only came out to go on stage and then back in the van and they were gone. The Who wandered around backstage in white jump-suits. I talked with Kris Kristofferson for a while and Joan Baez.

I spent a lovely hour with a sweet girl named Melanie who had a hit song about roller skates. Richie Havens gave me a pack of American Flag rolling papers, which I kept for years. I became friendly with a little-known performer called David Bromberg who played a well-received set, although he wasn't listed on the bill. I met him a few times back in the States over the next couple of years.

There are many memories of those five days, some crystal clear, some a little fuzzy. Jim Morrison arrived tired and jet-lagged, having flown in from San Francisco. I guided him on stage and he gave a fabulous performance. He wanted the spotlights turned off, which was arranged. When he was done, the crowd went wild but he walked up to me and said he didn't think they liked him! I literally pushed him back on stage to a thunderous ovation and he played another song.

Later that night, we sat leaning up against a caravan drinking beer. I told him I was going to drop out of college and was worried about being drafted into the army and being sent to Vietnam. I had dual citizenship and could legally be conscripted.

"Here's what you should do at the induction physical, Jon," he suggested. "Walk around the place with an invisible dog on a leash. Talk to him as if he was there. They'll think you're crazy and you'll get a 4-F!"

I thought that was great advice. I did act crazy at my induction physical and got rejected from the army a few months later. We talked for a couple of hours, drank some beers. He seemed like a lost little boy that night and less than a year later he would be dead.

Joni Mitchell played the piano and sang on Saturday, but just after she finished singing "Woodstock", a hippy named Yogi Joe burst on stage, grabbed her microphone and started yelling about the conditions in a campsite named Desolation Row. Joni's manager and I dragged him offstage and outside.

Joni followed and confronted him about showing respect for the artists. She was visibly upset and shaken. She returned onstage, quieted the crowd and ended her set with "Big Yellow Taxi."

So many great names I met and hung out with for a little time. I smoked a joint with John Sebastian before his long set. He was thrilled when Zal Yanovsky, his former guitarist made a surprise appearance on stage. Tiny Tim did a great version of 'There'll Always Be An England'!

Donovan was sweet and gentle. Shawn Philips was a really nice folk singer who played an impromptu set after John Sebastian. Ian Anderson of Jethro Tull told me he grew up down the street from where my grandparents lived in Streatham. I think he said his Dad had a barber shop there. Leonard Cohen happily embraced Joan Baez and they strolled around backstage together, catching up on things. I talked with Joan a little and told her I had burned my draft card the year before at a big demonstration. She hugged me.

And being so close to the musicians while they performed was incredible. To stand ten feet from Jimi Hendrix, while he did unbelievable things with his guitar. To hear Ian Anderson's flute before it went through the loudspeakers. The Moody Blues singing 'Nights in White Satin' under the starry sky. The new group 'Supertramp' had released their first album a few weeks before. They were very nervous! I met them again in Santa Monica several years later and spent a little time with them.

On the second day, I was onstage and looked down at the audience below. Right in the middle, in the front row was my friend Gordon, who I hadn't seen since we had said goodbye at Gatwick Airport two months before. I ran down the back stairs, forced my way through the crowd and we hugged each other.

"Was that you on stage a few minutes ago?" he asked.

"Yup, I'm sort of an assistant to the producer, Ricky Farr. You want to spend the rest of the festival back stage?"

He did, I got him a pass and we had a great time.

On Friday night, Chicago was the big hit, although I didn't like their music very much. I hung out with a couple of the guys from the Canadian group 'Lighthouse' and we smoked some pot and drank a few beers. Their set went over very well.

It was cold that night and the lead singer of Procol Harem commented on it. Mungo Jerry was there that night, but for some reason he decided not to play.

Saturday was a great day and night with performances by Miles Davis, Ten Years After (Alvin Lee was incredible!), Emerson, Lake & Palmer, The Who and Sly & The Family Stone. During

Sly's performance, another political dissident jumped onstage and Sly got so pissed off, he didn't do his encore.

Because the residents of the island were against having a bunch of 'hippies and freaks' on their hallowed ground, the authorities had forced the festival into a location which was far from ideal. The large field where the festival was held was surrounded by hills and most of the audience chose to sit there and enjoy the show, rather than spend a lot of money for tickets. In fact, after the second day the festival was declared a 'free event' and no more tickets were sold.

I had heard rumblings and arguments in the office and Ricky Farr and Jeff looked stressed out and worried. There was talk of not having enough money to pay the artists and it was unlikely that the staff, including me, would get paid. Some of the security guards had large dogs and one of them threatened to let him loose on Ricky if he didn't get paid!

Sunday was the last day and there was a terrific line-up. I had become friendly with two Americans who were called 'Good News'. They performed first, nervously but to a warm reception. Then Donovan, Pentangle, The Moody Blues, Jethro Tull, the amazing Jimi Hendrix, Leonard Cohen, Joan Baez and as the sun came up on Monday morning, Richie Havens ended his set and the festival singing 'Here Comes The Sun', which was breathtaking…

I did manage to get paid, although I would have done it for free! On Monday the roads were clogged with over 600,000 people trying to get on the few ferries to the mainland. I hitchhiked into Shanklin and spent a couple of days at a small hotel, waiting for most of the people to disperse, before making my way back to London.

The 1970 Isle of Wight Rock Festival was the last of the giant festivals. There has been a small festival held on the Isle of Wight every year since 2002 and there are music festivals all over the world. But there will never again be such a large gathering to hear so many eclectic groups with such an incredible energy... And I will always cherish being a part of it.

A boat delivery tale…

THE LONGEST DELIVERY

Part 1

Running for our lives

We were encouraged to deliver the new charter boats as quickly as possible to their island bases, with the captain making the final decision when to leave based on the weather. Normally a passage from the Charleston, S.C. base to Grenada, the southernmost of the Caribbean island chain, would take about fourteen days – this voyage took five weeks…

We left on November 22nd, 1994 aboard a new 44' Beneteau Oceanis, the flagship of the fleet. My best friend Chuck was first mate, a South African in his late twenties named Pat was second and we had another crew who had agreed to pay for his own food and flight home, Rob, a pleasant, impressionable young man in his early twenties. Having provisioned the boat, stowed the extra fuel cans and done a quick check on the systems, we headed out the breakwater into the Atlantic dawn. The forecast called for rising winds from the north in the afternoon, so we left early to be across the Gulf Stream before the northerly kicked up an ugly sea. With light winds we loped along at a sedate four knots and expected to be across and outside the Stream's influence within twenty four hours.

The Gulf Stream is a huge river of water about sixty miles wide that sweeps north along the east coast of America. In southern Florida, its western boundary is only a couple of miles offshore. It is over fifty miles of sailing due east to find the edge of the stream off Charleston. With this ocean river running at almost three knots, it is prudent to get across it as quickly as possible, as you will be continually carried north. Also, when storms come down from the north, in fact when the wind has any northerly component to it, huge irregular seas are whipped up quickly and suddenly.

It became a sunny day with some clouds starting to form to the north. The crew seemed to be meshing well and later that day as we entered the Gulf Stream, the water immediately turned a darker blue, as it normally does. I instructed the helmsman to steer five degrees south to counteract the strong northerly current and went below to check the thru-hull fittings.

After an hour rummaging in the bilges and doing some final stowing, I came back into the cockpit and as always, did a quick 360 degree scan of the horizon. Apparently nobody had been looking to the north and I could not believe what I saw…

Stretching from the west to the east far on the horizon and reaching up probably fifteen thousand feet was an unbroken wall of huge, dark, green-tinged clouds, with intermittent lightning flashes lighting up the inside of the clouds. I grabbed my binoculars and could see that in front of this broiling, chaotic mass, the waves were quickly being built up and were bearing down towards us.

"Bloody hell, hasn't anyone noticed what's on the horizon?" I demanded.

The crew turned their heads in the direction I was looking and their mouths fell open.

"No skipper, we were talking and chatting and I guess no one looked around for the last hour or so."

A complete 360-degree scan of the horizon is required every fifteen minutes by me. At this early point in what was to be one of the most memorable deliveries of my career, I wasn't about to alienate anyone by casting blame.

"Right. Pat, get the jib rolled in, Rob and Chuck, get the main down – NOW!"

I moved behind the wheel and turned on the engine. We were still in the Gulf Stream and with this fast-moving storm I knew the waves would become dangerous very soon. Many lives have been lost out here in a northerly and I had no idea how much wind was packed into this monster.

With the sails furled I ordered the crew to batten down all the hatches and portholes and secure all gear above and below decks. I told them to prepare for a drop in temperature and dress accordingly. Safety harnesses and tethers were mandatory. Pat thought I was over reacting and I had to yell at him to do as I commanded.

We all sat in the cockpit mesmerized as the front marched toward us. The clouds reached as high as you could see and the lightning flashes were like a snake's flickering tongue. It looked like the end of the world was about to engulf us.

A half-hour later the huge nor'easter was upon us. Within seconds the temperature dropped twenty degrees, the wind jumped from ten knots to thirty, the sky darkened, the rain came crashing down and six foot waves slammed into the boat. We were only a few miles into the Gulf Stream but with the strong wind the seas were continually building.

Deciding that it could be suicide to continue heading east in an untested boat with an untested crew, I spun the wheel to starboard and turned south into the waves, with the wind behind us. The boat was difficult to control under power and kept veering off course as waves from all directions tossed us about. I called to

Chuck to unfurl the jib halfway and when that was accomplished, I turned off the motor and the boat surged along at six knots, much easier to control.

In a 'regular' storm at sea, even though the waves may grow large, they generally move in one direction, being blown by the wind. But in the perverse Gulf Stream, the fast-flowing current meeting the high winds head-on over a relatively shallow sea bed, can cause irregular waves, triangular, even 'square' in shape with no distinct pattern or rhythm. It's very bouncy, very uncomfortable and very, very dangerous.

With Pat and Rob below, Chuck and I discussed our options. Chuck was a professional fishing boat captain with not much sailing experience, although he had accompanied me on our adventurous sail to Belize on my Gemini 30 catamaran the year before. He went below and got a marine weather forecast. NOAA weather had been caught a little unawares by the severity of the storm and were now calling for thirty-forty knot winds and twelve to fourteen foot seas in the Gulf Stream for the next twenty four hours! This was no place to be.

The violent sea conditions made access to the inlets on the coast impossible, so we decided after much discussion to head for Hilton Head Island where Port Royal Sound offered a large bay to enter and a slightly protected land mass to get into the winding Intracoastal Waterway and safety.

The seas were very confused by now and occasionally a rogue wave would come hissing down on us and inundate the cockpit and helmsman. Sometimes, we would be steering with water up to our knees as the scuppers struggled to drain the hundreds of gallons trapped in the large aft cockpit.

It was cold, wet, uncomfortable and scary. It was also getting dark, although the lightning would occasionally show us triangular waves with the tops being blown off in a welter of spray and spume. The hours dragged on with no let-up in the ferocity of the storm. Using my hand-held GPS, we set a course south-south-west and eventually found ourselves out of the Gulf Stream and in relatively calmer seas. We had calculated that we would be off Port Royal Sound by about 1:00 a.m. and we were.

Chuck fished the Sound every day as a commercial captain and I had operated my parasailing boat there for two summers, so we knew the waters well. But neither of us had seen it in these conditions. The Gulf Stream runs closer to shore here and the marginally protected waters of the Sound were wild and confused.

There were numerous shoals and we drew on all our knowledge to head down the middle and into the Intracoastal Waterway. In the pitch black and pouring rain the only illumination was a split second of lightning which for a brief moment showed where we were.

I radioed ahead on the VHF and got a response from a security guard at Skull Creek Marina on the north end of the island. He couldn't believe that there was a boat out there in these conditions, but he knew Chuck and me and he promised to turn on all the marina lights and meet us at the dock.

It wasn't easy bringing the boat safely alongside in the strong wind, but I managed it and with relief we tied up and turned off the engine. Chuck's sister came to pick us up at 3:00 a.m. and leaving Pat and Rob to dry out, we headed home for a hot bath and meal.

The first part of the delivery was over. But there was more adventure, much more to come.

Part 2

Escapades

The storm was still blowing the next day and I called the office in Charleston. The owner, Charles told me to use my own discretion and wait it out until I decided it was safe to head offshore again. We motored the boat over to Chuck's girlfriend's dock on Daufuskie Island, an hour away. Jan lived in a little cabin on the Intracoastal and was glad to have her boyfriend (and the rest of us) around for a while.

We spent a lazy week on the island as the storm blew for four days and the Gulf Stream kicked up bigger and bigger seas. A hurricane had also formed around the same time in the Gulf of Mexico and had blown east across Florida. This, combined with the nor'easter, created weather conditions that made being on the ocean untenable for days. Finally we decided to continue on the protected Intracoastal Waterway. We didn't want to get too far south, as it would mean beating further to windward out in the Atlantic in order to get to the elusive trade winds about four hundred miles offshore.

One sunny morning we left the ramshackle dock and headed toward Savannah with an extra crew member aboard. Jan had always wanted to do an ocean passage and had dreamed about being on the Caribbean island of Bequia on a Christmas Day. Although she didn't have enough money for return airfare and although I didn't tell the boss, circumstances proved it to be a wise decision.

Just south of Savannah we went aground, a fairly common situation in the sometimes shallow waterway, especially on a boat with a six-foot draft. With much forward and reverse and spinning the wheel, I got us off and we continued on our way.

The next day we headed down the Vernon River, out Ossabaw Sound and into the Atlantic. The seas looked relatively calm and as we crossed into the Gulf Stream with a westerly wind we were already two weeks into the trip and glad to be back at sea.

Even though it was strictly forbidden by the insurer, Lloyds of London, and unbeknownst to me, the crew had stashed several bottles of wine and spirits aboard and with Jan's superb culinary skills we merrily made our way four days out to the trade winds and turned south.

The sailing was superb, the nights were full of stars and meteors and we were a well-knit crew having a great time. One glorious sunny day the winds dropped for a couple of hours and we dove overboard in the middle of the Atlantic. It is an awesome and scary feeling to be splashing around with miles of water underneath and huge fish (and shark) lurking!

I had decided to sail past the Virgin Islands and head down the Caribbean chain on the leeward side of the islands, where we would be able to see each island and stop to provision if needed.

A day out of Tortola, while Pat was on the wheel the steering suddenly stopped working. I opened the inspection hatch and found that a misaligned block had caused the stainless steel cable to part. We did not have a replacement on board and no way to jury-rig it. We un-shipped the emergency tiller and slid the end over the square fitting at the head of the rudder post. Although awkward, it did provide control and we proceeded south – for about fifteen minutes. Then the weld on the tiller sheered off and the emergency steering was useless.

We tried steering with the sails and achieved some success, but it was a zig-zag course and pretty uncontrollable. Eventually, we cobbled together an ingenious series of rope and chain pulleys and using the jib winches, managed to steer the boat within an acceptable twenty degrees each side of our intended course.

Each hour brought us a little closer to Tortola where The Moorings had their main Caribbean base and eventually I managed to raise them on the VHF. They said they would send a boat to tow us in and six hours later we were tied up at the base. They begrudgingly said they would fix our problem but it would take at least a day.

I headed over to see my old friend Mrs. Ethlyn Burke who owned the 'It-Go Car Rental Company' in Roadtown. I rented a beat-up Jeep and loading the crew aboard took them on a tour of the island I knew so well. It was good to get off the boat and we reveled in the beautiful greenery.

In the early evening we headed back to Roadtown and Pat and Rob asked to be dropped off at a local bar. I told them we'd be heading south early the next morning and not to drink too much. They had no intention of listening to me...

After a great dinner of chicken rotis, Chuck, Jan and I had a glass of wine in the cockpit and turned in early. I was deep asleep when there was a loud knocking on the hull and a flashlight played over the boat.

"Cap'n White, Cap'n White, you on board, sah?"

I stumbled up the companionway steps grabbing a pair of shorts on the way. The flashlight was turned on me and I glanced at my watch – it was 2:00 in the morning and there were three people on the darkened dock, two of them wearing police uniforms! A large policeman was tightly holding the arm of my dripping wet crew member Pat.

"Hello, Constable, is there a problem?" I sleepily asked, although it was apparent there was.

"Yassuh, dere is a problem. Is dis mon a member of your crew?"

117

he asked, shining the light in Pat's face. He looked sheepish and scared.

"Yes, he is. What's happened?"

"Is dere another member of the crew, name of Rob?"

"Yes sir, there is, what have they done?"

By this time Chuck and Jan had thrown on some clothes and were in the cockpit. Pat, on the dock was weaving a bit, his eyes red, his clothes wet, obviously quite drunk.

"Well, Cap'n, seems your crew are in a lot of trouble, dey done damaged some property and ah found dis mon here makin' love to a lamp post!"

"Ah, blimey, well, I'll take care of them and bring them to the station tomorrow," I replied hopefully.

"No sah, dis mon's coming back to jail wit us and he'll be put with de other mon until de judge decides what to do wit dem. You be at the station at 8:00 a.m., Cap'n. Dis a serious offense on our islan'."

Pat looked pleadingly at me and Chuck started to protest but I shut him up quickly.

"Very well, Constable, I will be there and we'll sort this out."

Chuck, Jan and I sat in the cockpit under a brilliant moon and had a glass of wine then got a couple of hours sleep. As we ate breakfast at the Moorings Base, the general manager came over and asked why there were police on his docks in the early morning hours. It was important not to ruffle any feathers because my boss didn't want the lucrative delivery contract to go to another company in the bidding next year. I told him it was probably a misunderstanding and we were going to straighten it out in a few minutes.

"Good," he said, as he abruptly turned away "your steering will be fixed this morning and we need your boat off the docks."

Chuck and I found our way to Police Headquarters and after being frisked were shown to a small cell block already heating up in the island sun. The miscreants were in one tiny cell, fast asleep on bunk beds, snoring off their drunken spree.

"Hey, wake up, both of you," I called to them.

Sleepily they opened their eyes, looked around unbelievingly and sat bolt upright. Obviously this was not a wise move as they both grabbed their heads and started massaging their temples. Suddenly they realized they were not on the boat but in a very small jail cell, on the wrong side of the bars!

"Oh my God, what did we do?" cried Pat. Rob just sat there in quiet shock.

"That's what I want to know," I replied. "I've been talking with the arresting officers and now I want to know exactly what you remember."

"Well, we went to a few bars and had a lot to drink," said Pat.

Rob groaned as he remembered.

"Then we headed back to the boat and I remember peeing on a lamp post."

I could tell Pat remembered more than he was telling me and asked Rob if he had any recollection?

Pat shot him a look, but Rob was very scared now and told me what he could remember.

"I think we broke into a couple of cars and took some things. Then Pat wanted to steal a car to drive back to the base and we tried to get one started but I think – oh God, did it really roll into the sea?"

Rob was horrified and Pat looked a little contrite but still acted defiant.

"Shut up, Rob," he hissed. "I don't remember anything, what do the cops say?"

"OK gentlemen, this is what they told Chuck and me before they let us in here to see you. They found Pat with his arms around a lamp post in Roadtown, humping and grinding it, yelling that he wanted more mushrooms. You, Rob, were trying to pull him off as the police car came up. Then they apparently followed a path of destruction back through the town.

"There was a Suzuki Jeep that had been rifled with, the hand brake had been released and it had rolled down the bank and is now being winched out of the Harbour. There were three cars in the small parking lot near the bazaar which had each been broken into, several items had been stolen from the cars (a couple of which, two cassettes, were found in your possession) and one of you had taken a stolen lipstick and written obscene graffiti on the cars. You also broke a rear-view mirror and did some other minor damage..."

"No, we didn't, it wasn't us," said Pat defiantly. Rob sat on the upper bunk in a daze.

"I hate to tell you this, Pat but the police have found a couple of witnesses and they're going to take your fingerprints as soon as Chuck and I leave."

"Well, they'll probably just kick us off the island," said Pat, still unaware of how serious his situation was.

"No, mate, it's not quite as simple as that. Tortola is a tight-knit community and they don't stand for this kind of behavior on their island, especially when it was done by yachties to locals. The Jeep belonged to a prominent businessman and the other cars are owned by well-known people on the island. Theft of any kind is treated harshly here and vandalism is not tolerated. You are both in very serious trouble and the Chief Inspector told me you will be lucky to get off with two years in jail and it's not a nice jail, here on this island…"

Pat's whole demeanour changed and he started to cry.

"Get me out of here, Captain, please, just get me out of here."

"I don't know if I can but I'll see what I can do. Rob, give me your parents phone number, you too, Pat."

A guard came in and told us we had to leave as the men were to be arraigned and fingerprinted. We could come back in the early afternoon.

Rob was crying by now too but I wasn't angry with him and tried to reassure him. Pat was the instigator as I had seen a couple of times on the passage down. Rob was very impressionable and was taken in by Pat and his devil-may-care attitude. They both looked devastated and scared as Chuck and I left.

I went back to the Base and called my boss in Charleston. Apparently, The Moorings had already called him and he had some idea of what was going on.

"Listen, Jon. You need to completely disassociate yourself from Pat and Rob. Their behavior could jeopardize the long-standing relationship I have with The Moorings and you're just going to have to leave them, find another crew and get the boat to Grenada. It's been a month already and the boat is booked for a New Year's charter."

"But Charles, give me twenty-four hours, let me at least see if I can get them a lawyer, let their parents know."

Even though I was disgusted by their actions and furious with them for their disregard for other people's property, I was haunted by the look of utter despair on their faces, especially Rob.

"No, you're to have nothing more to do with them. Find a crew to help you and Chuck get the boat south and get the hell out of there. I'm going to deal with The Moorings brass from this end."

"I'll see if I can find another crew. I'll call you later."

A plan was brewing in my mind as I placed a long-distance collect call to Rob's parents in Vermont. As I explained the situation, Rob's mother started crying. She insisted her son had never done anything like that before. I told her that he was very impressionable and was following Pat's bad example. I explained the severity of the situation and told her I would call her back when I had met with a solicitor. She was very grateful and kept thanking me over and over.

When I called Pat's parents in South Africa, they didn't seem too surprised and told me they'd send whatever money was needed to get him out of this scrape. Apparently it wasn't the first time he'd done something like this. I told them I doubted money would solve the situation, he was in serious trouble. I said I'd give the solicitor their contact information and hung up.

"Seems like they've got lots of money and think they can buy his way out of this," I told Chuck. "Different reaction than Rob's parents. They're teachers and just average folks."

"Well," said Chuck. "This island's pretty corrupt; maybe Pat's parents can buy him out?"

I didn't want to leave them so far from home without any legal help but I had been ordered to get off the island as soon as I had another crew. I wanted twenty-four hours to see what I could do. And I had a plan...

Part 3

A Bequia Christmas

Chuck, Jan and I drove to my friend Mrs. Burke at the car rental.

"Are yah leavin' us now, Cap'n Jon?"

Mrs. Burke and I had a friendship that went back to the first time I sailed into Tortola, in 1989. When she was filling out the paperwork for my car rental we discovered we were born on the same day in the same year. From then on I always called her on our birthdays each year from wherever I was. And when I was in Tortola, no matter how booked she was she always found a car for me at 'de islan' rate'!

"No, Mrs. B. I need your help. A couple of my crew have landed in jail and I need to find them a good lawyer."

"Oooh, dose bad boys iz from your boat, eh? De whole town know 'bout what dey did las' night. Why, dey broke in mah fren Ida's car! Oohh, dey in BIG trubble, dem two!"

"Yes, Mrs. B. They are in big trouble and I'm embarrassed and humiliated by their behavior. But I promised their parents I'd do what I can, and that's why I'm asking you."

"OK, Cap, de bes' lawyer on de islan' is Jeremy Jones, he done studied in Englan' and he's family. Lemme call him an' see if he's willin' to help."

She went into her office and five minutes later a meeting had been arranged for later that day. Now I had to find the crew member I needed to make a compliment of three, the minimum required for Lloyd's of London insurance in order to do a paid delivery for The Moorings.

But this was the height of the charter season and every available crew member with the slightest sea experience was working. I had Chuck as first mate and I had a very willing, experienced sailor (Jan had just spent nine days in the Atlantic with us) sitting across from me…

I phoned Charles and told him I thought I had a crew but wouldn't know until the next morning. He wanted us out of there right away but he knew it wasn't going to be easy to replace Pat or Rob.

"Look, Charles. Chuck and I ran into this experienced crew who needs to get back to the States soon but she has a few days off. If you'll pay her plane fare back to Savannah from Grenada, I think I can convince her to sail down to Grenada with us…"

"OK, Jon, that's fine, just get her on board and there'll be a ticket waiting for her in Grenada."

I came smiling back to the table and told Chuck and Jan that my plan had worked, Jan was now the official third member of the crew and the company was flying her home! She threw her arms around me and we had a few more beers as we waited to meet the lawyer.

He was a tall, distinguished man in his mid-fifties and his island lilt was modified by the years he had spent studying law in England. I told him that I had studied at the College of Law in Guildford and we had an instant connection. We discussed what had happened and it was his opinion that the boys would probably get jail time, but "let us go and meet them and see."

We drove to the jail where a morose and subdued Pat and Rob were sweating in their tiny, hot cell. They immediately jumped up and Pat started crying again. I introduced them to their lawyer, told them I had spoken with their parents and that there was nothing more I could do. Pat had forfeited his plane fare home and they were on their own. Chuck and I had gathered their belongings from the boat and had left them with the authorities at the police station.

We shook hands all around through the bars. Rob was embarrassed and apologetic and even Pat, with all his bravado, couldn't look me in the eye. We left them to their fate and Mr. Jones.

The next morning I called Charles, told him that Jan had agreed to crew with us and that the steering had been fixed. We cast off ten minutes later, heading south for the final four hundred mile passage down to Grenada. It was December 23rd, the sun was shining and the winds pushed us past Virgin Gorda southwards at a glorious six knots on a sparkling Caribbean sea.

Two days later, as the sun rose in my eyes I steered the boat east toward the small and beautiful harbor on the Island of Bequia in the Grenadines.

I called for Jan and Chuck to come on deck as I needed help with the sails. They both sleepily stumbled into the cockpit, and followed my outstretched hand as I pointed to the island three miles off.

"Merry Christmas, Jan. There is Bequia just for you on Christmas Day. May all your dreams come true…"

I found out much later through the professional sailor's 'grapevine' that Pat and Rob had spent two months in jail, paid for the damages and paid the Tortola government an undisclosed sum for their release. Or rather, their parents did…They were kicked off the island and told never to return.

Many years after when Joell and I were based in Tortola for the charter boat show, I met some younger delivery skippers who I didn't know. We sat around drinking beer and spinning yarns. It wasn't long before one of them started talking about this crew member who years ago had been arrested for making love to a lamp post. That delivery adventure had become a legend in certain circles…

HITCH HIKING TO CALIFORNIA

It was early summer of 1974 and I had three months before I was due to leave America on the QE2 to move back to England. I had a few hundred dollars in my pocket and decided to hitchhike to California. I left New Hope, Pennsylvania with a pack on my back, a couple of joints and a feeling of unbounded adventure.

The journey west was a blur – truckers picking me up and dropping me off in god-forsaken towns in Indiana, Ohio, Nebraska. Occasional hippies with somewhere to crash and some good pot and wine. An angry cop in Arizona who didn't like my long hair or funny accent, me standing on an entrance ramp in the middle of the desert. He would throw me in jail if I was there when he came back from his cup of coffee down the road. Frantically I waved at the few cars coming onto the highway, finally got picked up by some bad dudes in a pickup truck, but they'd never met a foreigner, so all was cool.

The final stretch was oh so magic! Two cute hippy girls in a psychedelically painted VW bus, heading to their little house near Riverside. I made it to California in style, every hitchhiking man's dream…California was a haze, had fun in Santa Monica, partied in Venice, met some strange people and then headed back east.

In Barstow I got picked up by a young army guy in a mustard-coloured Sunbeam Tiger, the rare one with the V8 engine. We hurtled down the highway and sped through the night. He had a great sound system and some wicked weed. We took turns driving and I still remember fishtailing around bends in the mountain roads, the Grateful Dead wailing, the twin exhaust pipes roaring, tyres squealing and us howling with delight.

Coming down the Rockies at about 80 mph, the car started to pull to the right. I pumped the brakes and brought the little car to a screeching stop, an evil smell coming from the right front wheel.

Pulled the car off the road, took the wheel off and found the wheel bearing had frozen.

We were in the middle of nowhere, miles from any town. We took the wheel bearing off and he got a ride to the nearest town. Chances were he'd have to wait until the bearing could be sent out, unless they had one in the town – unlikely.

I settled down for a long wait. With the car jacked up, I decided to look under it, just my natural curiosity. I noticed some wrapped bundles tucked up under the rear wheel wells. I pulled one out and opened it. No wonder he had such good weed – there were about 50 pounds of it stuffed under the car! Now I always like a bit of adventure but the thought of a friendly cop stopping by to check out the problem with the little foreign sports car and the strange looking hippy and just what are those bundles under the wheel wells..?

I didn't stay around to find out. Stuck out my thumb and headed east, quick as I could...If you ever get to read this, I hope you got your car fixed and made a ton of money but can you blame me for splitting? And I'll be glad to pay you for the few joints I took from your stash – whoa, that was good stuff!

A CRUISING EMAIL

September 15, 2004

We have been in San Andres Island almost two weeks - two exciting, hot, frenetic weeks working on the boat. This little island 400 miles west of Colombia and 100 miles east of Nicaragua is a holiday destination for mainland Colombians and is also a duty free zone. So we have been buying lots of stuff necessary for chartering!

Last week we moved the boat from the anchorage to a funky little marina on the beach, complete with rickety old wooden docks, a beach bar, palm trees and tropical fish swimming around the boat. The owner, Tonino, is a very cool young guy, who besides being a medical doctor, is also the scion of a powerful and wealthy Colombian family. He is thrilled to have our large boat at his small marina!

As there is some petty theft here, he keeps three mean pit bulls tied up during the day and at night they are leashed on the docks, so we feel very secure. Every morning Sailor and I go for a walk on the beach, away from the dogs. However, sometimes they see him and they go nuts!

Two days ago, we were strolling along, Sailor keeping on the edge of the water, when this white streak raced by me and in a flurry of sand and sea, grabbed Sailor by his right haunch and started to toss him around. One of the nasty dogs had freed his rope and wanted Sailor really bad. Our poor little guy was yelping, I was screaming and hitting the pit bull to no avail.

The night watchman rushed over and started hitting the dog with a stick, but he wouldn't let Sailor go. A couple of seconds later an old man came running and huffing down the beach, drew back his arm and with a mighty swing landed a resounding punch on the pit bulls head. He fell over, letting Sailor go.

I gathered him up and ran yelling back to the boat. Joie took over and her experience as a zoo-keeper and volunteer for Wild Life Rescue came into play. We could only see one bite mark on his back and we watched him for a short time. He gradually went into shock, but could stagger around a bit. A few minutes later, Tonino's wife Victoria came to the marina and hearing of the problem rushed onto our boat. She has a Schnauzer that Sailor plays with and she loves dogs.

She called her vet immediately on her cell phone and literally ten minutes later, he was aboard the boat and expertly examined our little guy. Oscar knew what to look for and under Sailors thick fur, found two more deep large bite wounds. He gave Sailor an anaesthetic shot and cleaned, disinfected and sutured the wounds. He was confident there were no internal injuries and, two days later, this appears so.

Sailor has been a bit groggy and definitely quiet, but he is eating and walking around. He can't climb the stairs yet, but this morning he smiled at us. The vet came again yesterday and gave him another shot of antibiotics. For his house (boat) call, all the work he did, the medications, suturing etc., he sheepishly asked for $8 U.S.

I looked at him sternly.

"Eight Dollars U.S?" I asked, incredulously.

"Si, Capitan, eez too much?" he replied nervously.

"No, no, Oscar – is not enough for all your work – here is twenty dollars and that is still cheap!"

It hasn't taken long for word of Sailor's injuries to spread up and down the beach and we have had a constant stream of visitors. We hear a tentative "Hola" and then a young lady or a couple of guys will ask after "El perrito, Say-lorr". We invite them aboard and Sailor is gently coddled as we make new friends. We have had gifts of fresh coconut bread, cakes and fish and everyone wants to help us any way they can.

Sailor will get better, he is a tough little bugger and loves the attention. The locals are glad that we will be here for another month and so are we. This morning I took Sailor out for a walk and he was fine, just a little slow moving. And what a fuss was made over him!! These people are genuinely warm, open-hearted and friendly - we have decided to stop being Gringos and want to be Colombians!

Sailor will be as good as new in a while and we are delighted to have so many new friends - although they ask after "Say-lorr" before they ask how we are doing!!

With much love
Jon, Joell and Say-lorr

THE TIME TRAVELER

In early 1982 I worked with a friend selling real and fake fur coats at various venues, including flea markets, gun shows and fairs. It wasn't something I was particularly proud of but it filled a gap and made a little money. It was at a fair that I came across a 'handwriting' analysis machine, a concept that had been around for years. You signed your name on a card, it was inserted into a slot, lights flashed, things whirred and fifteen seconds later a piece of paper with ten 'personality traits' was spit out. Of course, it wasn't real but they did hundreds a day and people loved them. This business was very successful and they were all over the fair circuits across the country.

I thought about the huge amounts of money being generated and contemplated how this could be done with integrity, providing people with something of value and interest for their dollar. One evening I was walking around a fair and there was a barker promising to guess your age. People were going up to him and giving him a dollar. If he was right within three years, you lose. If he was wrong, you'd get a little prize that cost him a quarter!

What all the players had in common was a birthday. Everyone has a birthday but how many people know what was happening in the world on the day they were born? Would anyone be interested? I knew I would be. I asked some friends if they would spend a dollar to find out what had happened on the day they were born. They all said yes…

I left after the fair closed and went back to my brother's apartment in San Francisco. I spent a few days seeing if this idea of mine was even viable.

Personal computers were becoming more sophisticated and available. I had a friend who was a computer whiz and at the time worked for George Lucas Films doing computer programming.

I asked him if it was possible to write a programme that, when I punched in a series of numbers (such as a birthday) would print specific pieces of information in the same place each time. He said it wouldn't be too difficult and he could do it. I spent days designing a layout based on the front page of an old newspaper. I thought of different categories that might be of interest to everyone.

I researched the price of pre-printed paper, a computer, a printer. I investigated the circuit for the large state fairs around the country and I borrowed enough money from my brother to put all this together and make it happen.

But it took time – in fact nearly six months of going to the San Francisco Library every day, sitting in front of a microfiche machine and researching over 50,000 copies of the New York Times and other newspapers going back to January 1, 1900. I looked for the main headlines and copied them down word for word.

I became a fixture in the little microfiche room on the second floor. After a while the librarians would have my next reel waiting for me when I showed up at opening time. I had reams of legal pads full of my scrawl.

I could have finished the research sooner but many times I became enthralled by what I was reading and got caught up in the world of long ago. I 'was there' when the Wright Brothers flew at Kittyhawk. I waited on the docks with anxious relatives for news of the survivors of the Titanic. I watched the political chess game in Europe turn into the horror of World War 1.

I read of the millions of boys, a whole generation dying in the trenches. I reveled in the Roaring Twenties and lived through the collapse of the economy in the Great Depression.

I learned how FDR helped solve the problem of unemployment with the New Deal and Public Works. I read in disbelief of the rise of the Fascists in Germany, of Hitler's crushing destruction of Europe, of the concentration camps that few outside of them believed existed.

I read aghast of the effects of the only two atom bombs ever used against humanity at Hiroshima and Nagasaki. I saw the Marshall Plan rebuild Germany and lay the foundation for the industrial giant it is today. And the fifties, when there was relative peace and prosperity.

The assassination of JFK, the problems in Indo-China that became the Vietnam War. The Man on the Moon, Woodstock, the marches and demonstrations against the war (of which I was a part), the whole history of the U.S. and the world was available to me and I was immersed in it and wrote it all down.

I bought my first computer for $3000, a big IBM that had capacity for two 720K floppy disks! I remember the salesman asking me,

"Do you want a green screen, sir, or an orange one?"

You had a choice in 1982. No colour, just green text or orange. Graphics – no, they weren't available then and no one had heard of the internet. I bought a dot matrix printer, state-of-the-art, which could print one page of information in about thirty seconds and used paper with holes on the side to advance it. My friend wrote the programme and after some trial and error, he got it to print the data in the spaces on my pre-printed paper entitled 'The Birthday Chronicle'.

I acquired the federal trademark for the name and copyrighted the programme and information. I discovered two years later when Hallmark stole my idea that it's easy to get around copyrights and trademarks, especially if you're big business.

134

I spent two months at Grant's apartment painstakingly typing in all the information I had gathered. And then it was finished and it was good, very good. I would type in a birthday, the computer would hum and whirr and thirty seconds later the printer would deliver a one page replica of the front page of an old newspaper.

The information included three major news headlines, who was President and Vice-President, a comparison cost of a dozen staples including a house, car, loaf of bread, what was the most popular song, who won the world series and a few more.

I practiced for my friends and family. It was a huge hit! I thought I might be on to a big money-maker and got myself booked into several of the biggest state fairs around the country.

I built a collapsible booth, a custom counter and backdrop. I bought an ancient and rusty orange Dodge van with a three-speed manual transmission, squeezed my booth and equipment inside and headed south to the Orange Show in San Bernadino County, near L.A., my first introduction to the public.

I sold 1600 print-outs in a week for a dollar a piece and was pumped! I learned a lot at that show and made a few changes to my booth. I built a large clock that ran with the hands spinning backwards and hung it on the back of the booth – it drew a lot of attention. I called myself 'The Time Traveler; I'll Take You Back In Time For a Dollar'.

That summer of 1983 was exciting, exhausting, entertaining and very, very profitable. I criss-crossed the country, following the circuit. I would show up in a capitol city, Sacramento, St. Louis, St. Paul, Albany, Albuquerque and many more. I always reserved a 10 X 10 space in one of the buildings housing exhibits and different items for sale. My booth and equipment only took an hour to set up.

And I always had curious exhibitors coming over as soon as the big clock started spinning backwards. I would usually do a couple of hundred print-outs before the fair even started!

But I was totally flabbergasted when the doors opened to the public at my first really big show in Milwaukee. Within an hour, there must have been a hundred people crowding my booth, calling out their birthdays. I worked feverishly, joyously for twelve hours a day, occasionally dashing off to the bathroom and dashing back to find more and more people wanting print-outs.

Some folks would come back the following day with a list of birthdays, twenty or fifty, that they wanted for birthday gifts. The dollar bills piled up under my counter – many days I did over a thousand print-outs. I bought another computer as a backup and two printers. I ordered 20,000 sheets of paper to be delivered to the next fair…

Word got out and I was interviewed on local news stations. And then, at the show in Milwaukee I was approached by a man who wanted to do this himself. He had watched the lines of people eager to pay me a dollar for a piece of paper that cost me less than a penny.

"Would you sell me a copy of your computer program?" he asked the third night of the show, as I was closing up.

I told him I would think about it and he should come back tomorrow. That evening in my hotel room, after counting my money, I figured out how much I could potentially make with this business over a season. I also realized that I had perhaps three years before the concept would be copied by other people, there would be similar programmes developed and the market would be saturated.

If I sold my computer data to other people, I would be hastening the saturation but if I didn't grab all I could from this business, other people would...

The next evening he returned. I told him I would create a detailed manual and sell him two sets of disks for the princely sum of $15,000. He readily agreed and I was dumbfounded! I told him I would work on the manual after the show ended. I had a week before the next show and he gave me his phone number.

After the very successful show ended, I stayed with a young lady I had met and spent three days at her house writing a manual on how to boot up, operate and update the programme. I made more copies of the floppy disks and a few days later we met at his bank. I gave him a total of ten floppy discs (lots of backups), the manual and a contract I had had a lawyer draw up outlining the terms of this business opportunity. He gave me $15,000 in cash.

It was a very good fair and the beginning of a trend that continued for two years as I spent the summers in the northeast and mid-west and the winters in Florida printing tens of thousands of Birthday Chronicles and selling over two dozen sets of programmes.

After the second year, it was apparent that the competition was building. More and more clones were out there and I knew my time was coming to an end. My programmes were now selling for only $5,000 and finally I sold the whole business, van, booth, legal rights to sell the programme, everything and walked away.

The final straw had come after I sent a proposal to Hallmark in Kansas City that I had a concept I thought would do well in their retail stores. I met with them, showed them my computer and programme and proposed a percentage deal where I would provide the software and they would buy the hardware and instruct each store owner how to operate it.

They initially expressed interest then wrote me a letter saying they had decided not to follow through with this. Six months later, I was in a Hallmark store and there was the exact set up I had suggested to them, the same computer and Tandy printer, a similar layout but they called it 'The Birthday Times'…

I called my lawyer, just furious but he wisely suggested I be happy with my success and let it go.

"They have dozens of lawyers, Jon. They'll tie you up in litigation for years and it will cost you a fortune. In the end you may not get a penny. It's really not worth it…"

I was angry and felt cheated but I knew he was right. I let it go and eventually moved on to another success – the SR2 Simulator Ride.

Years later, my wife Joell and I were in a mall in Palm Beach, Florida. In the center was a booth offering all kinds of knick-knacks, plush toys and a computer programme called 'The Birthday Chronicle'. I remembered that I had sold a programme to a couple in Palm Beach, after one of the winter fairs I had worked. And here it was, still bringing in a few dollars. We walked on by, a smile on my face…

THE 'SPRAY'

After I sold my successful parasailing boat and business in 1994, I found myself hired as captain on a variety of boats on and around Hilton Head Island, South Carolina. For one summer I was one of the captains of the 'Spray', a 56' version of the famous sailing boat Joshua Slocum had sailed around the world singlehanded in the late 1800's – he was the first man to do this and his book remains a classic.

Three times a day the boat would embark up to forty-nine passengers for a two-hour sail in the waters off Harbortown. Usually the engine would stay on while the sails were up because she was a heavy boat with internal ballast and no keel and was difficult to maneuver in the best of conditions. With nearly fifty men, women and children aboard and only two crew I was always in a state of watchful alert. At the same time, I was entertaining the passengers with stories of Captain Slocum, getting some passengers to help raise the sails and looking out for the myriad other vessels in the area including jet-skis and ferries.

Usually everyone had a great experience, the kids loved helping raise the sails and steer and the weather was rarely an issue. However the South Carolina coast sometimes gets hit with sudden, nasty thunderstorms in the early afternoon and occasionally the wind can go from ten to forty knots in a matter of minutes.

One midsummer day, the boat was full of tourists from all over the world anticipating a pleasurable sail along the shores of Daufuskie Island with the possibility of seeing dolphins. As I backed out of the dock (which had the best position in the harbor, right alongside the promenade) a couple of hundred families stopped to watch the ship. With her shiny black topsides and white trim, two varnished gaff-rigged masts and a full complement of passengers, she made an impressive sight.

I blew three blasts on the horn, the signal for a vessel backing out. I noticed briefly that the wind was blowing more from the south than usual but paid it little heed. My attention was riveted on getting us away from the dock and hard-a-starboard in the confined fairway without damaging the boat or my reputation.

After hauling the mizzen up quickly, I was able to use it to blow the stern around to starboard, then spun the large spoked wheel to port and eased her into forward. Slowly we gained way and motored sedately out of the harbor with applause from the passengers and cheers from the bystanders ashore. It was a lovely afternoon, blue skies and a ten knot wind from the south-south-east.

Within five minutes some kids had helped the crew raise the large gaff mainsail and set the two jibs and at a steady four knots heeled over slightly, I turned off the engine. Dolphins appeared and for ten minutes the guests were enthralled with their leaping, playful antics. Then they swam out to sea (dolphins, not guests!) and everyone settled down comfortably. For the next twenty minutes I explained who Joshua Slocum was and regaled them with some of his adventures – a couple of mine were added too!

Around two o'clock, it was time to gybe the boat and head back to Harbortown. The wind had been picking up and clouds had been rolling in for the past fifteen minutes. I turned on the motor to help with the gybe as the Spray was an unwieldy vessel when any maneuvering needed to be done. Most of Captain Slocum's journey was off the wind and his original Spray was only thirty-six feetlong but I still have a huge amount of respect for his boat-handling skills.

As we headed back the three miles, the sky darkened suddenly and dark, ominous clouds moved in quickly. Looking astern, I could see small waves building behind us and the wind suddenly shot up to around twenty knots. I called my two crew over and quietly told them to get the sails furled without alarming the passengers.

I struggled to turn the boat into the wind to get the sails down and the job was completed in about ten minutes, under a threatening sky and steadily building wind. Some of the passengers were looking a bit worried, especially when it started to sprinkle rain. I asked parents to take their children below and had one of the crew make sure the kids all had lifejackets.

Within a few more minutes the storm was upon us and the rain came thundering down. The waves picked up and the wind was howling. I kept smiling, reassuring my worried guests that this was part of the adventure and we'd be back at the dock in a little while.

Some of them requested life jackets and I had the crew provide them for everyone. No one panicked, they all seemed confident in me but I was having concerns about getting the Spray into her confined berth in a crosswind of forty knots in a small harbor.

I called my crew over again and told them to keep circulating among the passengers, most of whom were on deck and soaked through, making sure they were alright. I instructed the crew that as soon as we entered between the narrow breakwaters at the harbor entrance, they were to have lines ready to throw over the starboard side and I would radio ahead for assistance at the dock. With just a few minutes to go, I radioed the harbormaster and asked for help docking.

"Captain'" he replied, "can you come alongside the fuel dock and I'll be down to catch a stern line around a cleat?"

"No, I thought of that, it would definitely be easier but the wind will be directly astern and if the line isn't caught and tied immediately, I'll be blown down onto the docks and do a lot of damage. You know this boat's a pig to handle, especially trying to stop her in reverse."

"Right, I know that, I've driven the old beast! So what will you do?"

"Well", I said, "I really have no option but to get her into her regular slip, even though the wind will be blowing me sideways."

"I understand," he replied, "But you'll have one shot at it and if it's not perfect, you're going to damage the boat and the dock."

"Yes, I know that, but I've got a bunch of wet, scared people aboard and I need to get them ashore. Have some people standing by; I'll be coming through the breakwater in three minutes..."

In a loud, calm, authoritative voice, I asked for complete silence and told the passengers on the starboard side to keep their heads low as I needed to keep that side of the boat clear for the docking I was about to attempt.

I came through the breakwater as slowly as I could, bumping the engine in reverse, steering slightly to starboard as the stern slid sideways from the direction of the propeller thrust. In the bars and restaurants around the harbor, the large glass windows were lined with people watching this stately vessel come into the harbor with driving rain and forty knots of wind behind her underneath dark, scudding clouds.

The slip was to port about a hundred yards from the entrance and necessitated a tight, ninety-degree left turn to put her between the two dock pilings. In calm, benign conditions this took skill and patience and earlier that summer another captain had demolished the boarding steps when he misjudged his turn and the eight foot bowsprit speared the steps, dragged them along the dock and left them hanging impaled on the bowsprit!

My crew were ready, dock lines in hand and there were half a dozen helpers on the dock all in oilies, all dripping wet.

142

Looking behind me to gauge the full force of the wind I squinted through the rain, spun the wheel to port and jammed full throttle reverse to slow her down and kick the stern around further.

Everyone on board held their breath and it seemed that everyone ashore did too, those on the dock and those watching from the safety of the shore side establishments.

Had I timed it too soon, was I going to ram the bowsprit into the yacht tied up in the next slip? A quick turn to starboard and back hard over to port and she glided right between the dock pilings at two knots, with steerage way but too fast to stop her. With the engine at maximum rpm in reverse she slowed a little but the wind took the bow and forced it against the dock.

The crew had hung out all the fenders we had aboard and they took the strain, although two of them burst from the immense pressure (fenders, not crew!). The lines were thrown ashore and the stern line was caught and in a flash wrapped around a stout cleat. The Spray came to a shuddering halt, I let out my breath and started shaking with relief. A cheer went up from the passengers, from the guys on the dock and all around the harbor, people were banging on the windows and applauding!

The steps were placed next to the boat and one of the crew helped the guests off, while the other stood with the tip jar, hardly expecting any money after what was undoubtedly one of the scariest experiences for our drenched passengers. But apparently they were not scared too much and they all expressed confidence in the captain and crew as they stuffed fives, tens and even twenties in the tip jar!

As one tourist said, "That was a real sea adventure, we'll never forget it, thanks so much, Captain!"

I had brought the boat in safely and looking back over hundreds of docking maneuvers in many different vessels, this was undoubtedly my finest moment...

So, you made it to the end...assuming you didn't only read the last story!

The sequel is now available, as many people around the world asked for it; 'Everyone Said I Should Write Another Book'.

Feel free to drop me an email at **jonandjoell@gmail.com**

I now have a facebook fan page. Please 'like' me:

www.facebook.com/EveryoneSaidIShouldWriteABook

A review on amazon.com is also appreciated;

www.amazon.com/EveryoneSaidIShouldWriteABook

If any of you are offended by the occasional mention of recreational drugs, those stories were written about a time long gone, the sixties and seventies. I don't condone or encourage illegal drugs these days...

We're still very involved with SendOutCards, growing this wonderful business which each day makes the world a nicer place and will enable us to retire and sail the Caribbean again...

If you or anyone you know is looking for a fun way to create a part-time or a full-time income, please visit:

www.sendoutcards.biz/jollycards

And remember these words:

This is your life – it's not a rehearsal...carpe diem!

Made in the USA
Lexington, KY
22 August 2013